# The Wilderness Cabin

By Calvin Rutstrum

*The New Way of the Wilderness*

*The Wilderness Cabin*

# The Wilderness Cabin

Calvin Rutstrum

*Illustrated by Les Kouba*

*1961*

The Macmillan Company
*New York*

First Printing

The Macmillan Company, New York
Brett-Macmillan Ltd., Galt, Ontario

Printed in the United States of America

Library of Congress catalog card number: 61-9730

To FLORENCE, who in her devoted editorial journey through this manuscript has been compelled to linger long and wearily on the back trail to track down what modifies what.

C. R.

# Acknowledgments

My sincere appreciation for the use of the following photographs to: M. E. Alford of the Canadian Department of Northern Affairs and National Resources, Yukon River log cabin; R. F. Anderson, photographer, two-story wilderness cabin; O. J. Braa, Lake Superior, North Shore log cabin; Humphrey's Photo Art, Grand Marais, Minnesota, stockade type log cabin; Barney and Virginia Briggs, of Sherwood Forest Lodge, Brainerd, Minnesota, log cabin (Virgil S. Ross, photographer, Lake Hubert, Minnesota); Thomas M. Burris, early settler's log cabin; Mrs. Joseph Chapman, Lake Superior "Encampment" Forest log cabin; Nobel Clark, Saganaga Lake, wilderness log cabin; Condon-King Co., Inc., Firehood; Douglas Fir Plywood Association, plywood cabins and interiors; Austin Houck, Ontario Wilderness log cabin (Lennie A. Hogan, photographer); Lake Hubert (Minnesota) Youth Camps, log cabin; McCulloch Motors Corporation, chainsaw operations; Fritz Metzger, trapper's cabin, Manitoba Wilderness; Ouisconsin Fish and Game Club, semistockade cabin, Ontario Wilderness; Portland Stove Foundry, Franklin Stove; Lewis Rasmussen, Ontario Wilderness log cabin; Doris & George Schaub, Moosehorn Lodge log cabins, Sioux Lookout, Ontario; Vega Industries, Heatilator Unit; Rick Whitney and Don Lobdell, Rockwood Lodge, Grand Marais, Minnesota, log cabin.

# Contents

# 1

## The Cabin in Perspective

THE CABIN as a distinct American style, or as a means to a unique and rewarding way of life, is apparently here to stay. Its simple, elemental form in our complex modern civilization has retained its color and its meaning. It persists as one of the best of our living traditions.

While the modern cabin is often so elaborate as to be classified as a house, and the modern house, because of its owner's wish for simple living, can sometimes be mistaken for a cabin, the overlap has fostered, if anything, the basic architectural idea.

The influence of the pioneer's cabin is still very evident. We have retained much of the picturesque quality of the early cabins and some of their structural principles. Here the similarity seems to end.

Cabins built under pioneer conditions, contrary to modern-day needs, were for immediate shelter. There was little opportunity to indulge in architectural vanity. The task of pushing back the wilderness to make a living from the soil was a full-time job, and too often a grim one.

To begin with, the area around the settler's cabin usually was denuded of every tree as a precaution against the ever-present hazard of

1

Imagination and a sense of design are shown in this composite—from the cabin proper, to the porch design, to the control of the vegetation.

forest fires, and to provide a convenient fuel supply. Dirt was the extent of most roofing, and tarpaper a luxury. If split shakes—the pioneer's shingles—could be made, they furnished the best in roofs. Split shakes are no less highly prized for cabins today.

As a rule, in the early days, cabins were set directly on the ground, without suitable footings, and the walls were banked with dirt to ensure added warmth. If in rare instances lime or cement for concrete footings or foundations could be brought over long distances to these remote sections, it was most often regarded as a needless luxury.

Next best to concrete footings was setting the cabin on cedar posts set below the frost line. In time these decayed. Without proper footings, the cabins heaved out of shape because of frost and decay. The door and window frames forced out of line by heaving and settling prevented proper opening and closing of doors and windows. Chinking between logs, forced out by the shifting timber, had to be replaced from time to time. Roofs, under stress, leaked.

In early cabins the notching of wall logs was usually done on the upper side. But water pockets soon rotted the log joints.

Thus, the original log cabin of necessity was a hand-wrought product of the forest throughout. Its roof was made of closely fitted poles, bark and dirt, or hand-split shakes. The floor was made of split logs or dirt. If the owner was not too closely pressed to maintain his bodily existence, he smoothed the flat side of the split-log floor with an ax, adz, or broad-ax. His door was also made of split logs—the hewn flat side battened to hold the pieces of split logs together. Where nails were not to be had, or had to be hand-forged, he found it more expedient to dowel sections together; that is, he bored holes and drove home hardwood pegs. Boards, sawed from logs (whipsawed) by hand, were precious.

Such cabins have become significant and symbolic in our history. Certainly they were naïve and rude; but, given the existing tools and means, they were not the products of unskilled or inexpert hands.

Logs hewn out of the forest by the pioneer's ax provided the quickest and most economic means of obtaining shelter. Sawmill lumber and other factory-made building materials were a long way off, and even if he could afford them, the pioneer might have to wait weeks and months before they could be brought in by river boat or wagon. And the luxury of rail transportation was still only a dream of the future.

On the prairie, where there was no standing timber, the walls of cabins were generally made of sod, cut from the earth in squares and piled to wall height. The desert cabin was adobe—sun-dried mud brick.

Once a settler had decided where he was to clear land and plant his crops, the need for an immediate shelter was urgent. If his shelter was made of logs, he had no time for niceties, and generally left the bark on his logs. Before long, wood-borer worms under the bark, warmed by artificial heat, kept many a pioneer in a state of restless sleep by their ceaseless grinding. Falling sawdust from their boring was the housewife's continual despair.

Later as lumber began to come up the river on steamer, barge, or by wagon road, or appeared in quantity when the sawmills arrived, the primitive log cabin rapidly gave way to the "frame" cabin—a cabin made from dimensional lumber. In turn, the small cabin, both log and frame, gave way to the formal two-story house. There was a strong urge for the architectural look of the villages and towns that the settlers had left. Log cabins, where they persisted in small com-

An Early Settler's Cabin of Squared Timbers with Bark Roof

munities, became more refined, with roofs and floors of planed lumber. Actually, this was not so much a matter of continued use of logs for design as it was one of economy.

Efforts were made in the early days to refine log cabins, but, we may assume, more to ensure domestic comfort than to create a pattern of architecture. Peeling the bark from the logs was the first step toward refinement. The greatest effort at refinement was the squaring of timbers and the dovetailing of corners. Round logs even when peeled somehow became synonymous with austerity—failure to afford the more modern board structure. Board houses, or what we call "frame houses" today, had smooth walls that were strongly appealing to the early housekeeper.

The rare individual who expertly made a log cabin as an architectural pattern was not the rule but the exception.

Where, then, do we get our modern, highly developed log-cabin tradition?

Strictly speaking, the log cabin with peeled logs, of refined, lacquered and stained surfaces, close-fitting, underlog-notched joints, lumber and shingle roof, dressed-and-matched flooring, plus all the refinements offered by the lumberyard, hardware and plumbing dealer, is largely of recent origin. Unless this is recognized, one gets involved in structural notions and details that do not apply to the original log-cabin construction.

In the final analysis if we can combine modern adaptations to the refined log cabin without being overly squeamish about the new applications of concrete footings or foundations, factory-planed lumber, nails, commercial hardware, plumbing, electrification, built-in kitchens, air conditioners, and other mechanization and appliances, we still have a log-cabin structure that blends effectively with the forest, or for that matter with almost any terrain. This adaptability of the log cabin to blend with almost any natural surroundings alone justifies, I think, the building of a log cabin today. Even though present-day improvements are incorporated within it, we may still regard it with traditional sentiment.

Obviously there are other reasons to be considered for building a log cabin.

Dovetailed Corner Section of an Early Settler's Squared-Timber Cabin

Most cabins or, if you will, cottages and lodges strung through the wilderness and recreational areas of the world too often have interiors that in no way suggest the nature of the region in which they are situated but which they should certainly reflect. As you step through the door of many of these cabins, you find that the basic purpose and idea for building and living in that area have been forgotten. The

The utter simplicity of this cabin needs no special qualification.

spirit and true nature of the surrounding countryside have not been brought indoors.

Natural-log interiors, on the other hand, furnished to reflect the country in which they are built, have an enduring quality and charm as pleasingly right to the human eye as the growth of a tree.

Logs, as the backwoods' saying goes, may grow on trees, but the harvest is costly. In this day of high labor costs, you can make a fair estimate of the expenditure by considering that a log cabin, if commercially built, will involve about twice the investment of a frame cabin. This is on the assumption that you will build a highly finished cabin with peeled logs and expertly fitted joints. If you do all of the work yourself—and you can if you are at all adept in the use of tools —your cash outlay naturally will be far less. The value of your experience, too, will be worth more than the precious time you spend in its construction.

If you have the temperament of an artist, and less that of a mechanical or structural perfectionist, a log cabin will be satisfactory for you.

On the other hand, if you are a perfectionist your first serious log-cabin disillusionment may come when you discover that the logs in the walls are checking as they continue to season and dry. Much of this checking can be prevented if, at the time the logs are freshly cut, you remove the bark a width of about 2 inches along the top and along the bottom, the full length of the log, as you plan to have the logs lie positioned in the wall; then stockpile the logs and allow them to dry thoroughly. To some extent the checking will occur primarily at these scored areas. You can remove the remaining bark at the time you begin construction of your cabin.

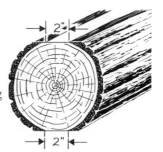

Partial Stripping of Bark to Localize Log Checking

Log shrinkage compels a few other considerations. You will have to allow for a space above the door and window frames, so that as the logs shrink and settle they will not be resting unevenly, or with crushing effect, on your doors and windows. (See Chapter 6.)

Owing to the checking that takes place in logs, care will be needed to keep log cabins free of vermin. The spiral checks that sometimes encircle logs may form openings that are not easily found in your later search for the mysterious exits and entrances of mice and insects.

If you love close tolerances, dislike imperfections, and suffer whenever you get a scratch on some priceless possession, a log cabin is not for you.

"Look once to see beauty, twice to be critical," says the artist. The beauty of the log cabin must be taken in at a glance. Paint your visual picture of a cabin with firm, broad strokes. The chances are that no one but yourself will ever see the natural imperfections that accrue with time. If, then, you choose the log cabin, don't let such imperfections weigh heavily upon your spirit.

Converts steeped in log-cabin tradition have led many of us to believe that anything but a log cabin in the woods is a form of structural heresy. That they have a point we must admit, when we look at those recreational frame structures that so often resemble the proverbial crackerbox.

Application of newly developed, rugged, and rustic materials have greatly changed this concept of jerry-building in frame-cabin con-

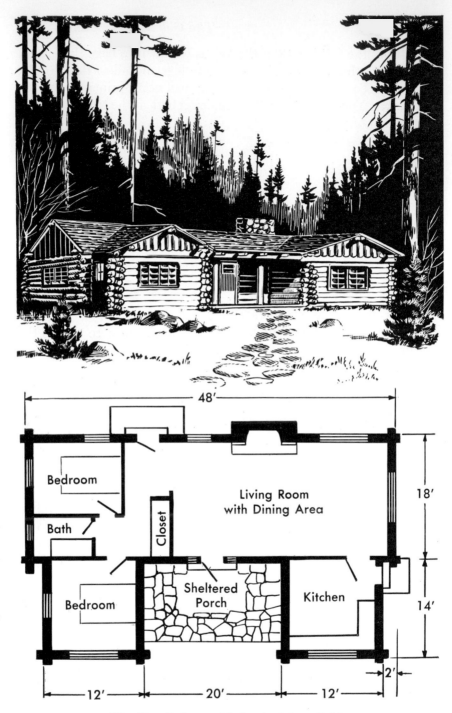

The Two-Bedroom Modernized Log Cabin

A Good Adaptation of the Two-Story Cabin

struction. Now it is possible to create with commercial materials a natural cabin that competes quite favorably with the log cabin, and in many instances where imagination and suitable materials are used even surpasses the log cabin in picturesque effect.

Structures with lopped-off eaves, thin narrow slatlike siding, or with a parsimonious application of other materials can hardly be called cabins in the traditional sense. They are no more than kin to the small houses or cottages so prodigally strewn on our overpopulated lake fronts. No matter how much imagination is used in the finish or the setting, such structures, in the true sense of the term, are not cabins.

We are sometimes told that a two-story structure cannot truly be a cabin. This opinion, I think, should be regarded with reserve. The two-story cabin has an excellent application in the Swiss chalet—a

9

The plywood ski-hut type of cabin needs a steep roof to shed snow.

structure I like to think of as a cabin. In some types, however, the two-story structure gets the form of a house. The two-story cabin needs only a more carefully thought-out architectural design. This point has been well borne out in adapting two-story cabins of proper materials to sites with extremely varied elevations, such as rockbound coasts, mountain slopes, riverbanks, and other split-level elevations.

We are generally on the right track to picturesque frame-cabin construction if we plan and build with rugged materials such as stone, timbers, rough-sawed heavy siding, split-shake or heavy shingles, and wrought iron. And we are almost certain of success if, in combining these materials, we adapt the low-gable roof design and broad chimney effect used so distinctively in the log cabin of tradition. Frame cabins can then be as pleasing and durable in natural appearance as the log cabin itself.

If the log cabin seems to have stolen the show by its imposing ruggedness and dignity of weight, it would seem that the frame cabin needs only the application of rugged materials to achieve the same success. Generally speaking, this is true. But despite the strong favor toward rugged, substantial cabin effects, we have in recent years come almost suddenly into an era when the basic concept of lightness rather than weight and ruggedness in construction is rapidly occupying an imposing place in the building of small cabins.

Lightness does not imply weakness or spindly construction, but rather greatly reduced material weight combined with strong structural principles. Laminated wood, for example, light in weight and surprisingly strong, has captured the imagination of designers and technicians, giving great emphasis to the idea of lightness.

The sweeping trend toward lightness in cabin construction today is achieved with plywood of great variety, wood-lamination-assemblies, and an increased use of gussets. (See illustration, page 29.)

The remarkable strength of fir plywood, coupled with the rapid, low-cost construction possible in the use of large plywood sheets, cuts down building expenses to a very significant degree. A roof covering made of plywood without additional roofing or shingles is in itself a substantial saving. But when you apply the same idea to walls that achieve both attractive exteriors and interiors with a single application of novelty-surfaced plywood sheets; to single floors of plywood that give a sound underfooting; and then, by virtue of plywood's great tensile strength and rigidity, when you cut down the support lumber

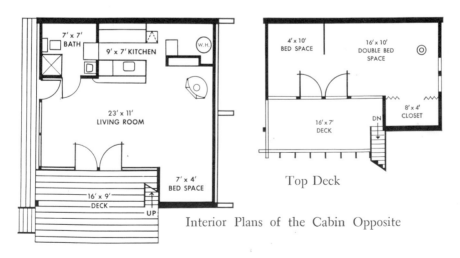

Interior Plans of the Cabin Opposite

by about half—economy in a day of high costs becomes so obvious, we must concede that the low-budget cabin today is the fir-plywood structure.

Plywood cabins, growing in popularity, will no doubt remain with us in an increasing variety of attractive designs and unique structural applications.

If in the past you hesitated between the log cabin and the rugged-frame or stone cabin as your ultimate choice, you are now faced with an additional choice—the plywood cabin. And it is altogether likely you may be attracted by its building advantages.

Any general new trend, such as the plywood cabin, allows for variations and compromises in construction and design. Plywood and laminated-wood cabins have been built exclusively of these materials. However, it should be kept in mind that plywood and wood lamination for trusses and support assemblies also lend themselves effectively in combination with other building materials—conventional lumber of all kinds, roofing and shingles, brick and stone.

In short, there is no particular theme that we must follow in the application of the plywood structure, or in the application of other general materials, for that matter. Effective combinations of materials usually work out better than strict adherence to one particular material. This applies to both interiors and exteriors.

Preassembled, ready-to-erect cabins are gaining wide favor. We shall see more of this with the passing of time. It is the quickest solution to acquiring a cabin. The prefabricated log cabin will be considered in the chapter on log cabins in general. We should distinguish between precut cabins and prefabricated or preassembled cabins. Precut cabins are simply the dimensional pieces of lumber cut to fit the cabin custom-built on the site. Prefabricated or preassembled cabins are in a sense cabins that have been built at the factory and then taken down in sections to be set up on the site. Actually, of course, the sections are created separately at the factory, the various sections when fitted together completing a cabin.

Almost every lumberyard represents a particular firm that makes preassembled cabins. The materials used are extremely varied in a wide choice of cabin designs.

# 2

## Insight into Sites

CONSIDERATION of where you hope to build your cabin implies close examination of your whole social and economic outlook. No matter how uninvolved or romantic you may be, there is a pretty good chance that your choice of site will depend on your family, if you have one, and certainly on your job, unless you don't have one. If you have neither family nor job, you can take off at once over the first alluring horizon of adventure.

Except where your cabin is to be deep in an unchanging wilderness, I urge you to give first thought to its resale value. If you are now about to toss this book aside with the remark, "This fellow has no sentiment," let me say, "Listen to some revealing facts."

My first cabin in the North, situated near a wagon road and a tumbling trout stream, has long since been buried under the ballast and asphalt of a four-lane highway.

My next cabin, in a vast game-populated evergreen forest fronting on Lake Superior's rockbound coast, has now been industrialized out of existence by a twenty-million-dollar taconite plant.

My third cabin, at the fringe of the Superior-Quetico Forest, on

Whole log complements greatly increase the effect of log siding.

an island a good two miles from shore, seemed relatively secure. It was routine to observe moose feeding in the shallows on the opposite shore and hear loons calling over a silent, moonlit lake. Within ten years of my building it, outboard-motor boats trailing water skiers roared past my door in disturbing numbers, cutting curves around the peaceful, island-strewn lake and driving the wildlife from its shores. If you have no objection to this sort of thing, you may stay. I sold out again, to rebuild elsewhere in solitude.

Higher resale value is about the only encouraging factor in these periodic moves from encroaching civilization. The increase in real-estate value may prove to be of no actual gain for you in cash unless you decide to move to a less inhabited region where land values have not yet skyrocketed. But on the whole, there is a strong likelihood that in cold cash you will have profited handsomely.

I have often been asked the question, "Does it really pay to own a cabin you can't get to except during extended vacations or long week-ends?"

I think it does pay. In the long run, taxes and interest on your investment are usually regained by increasing property values. The sheer joy alone of owning a cabin has a much-needed influence on your mood and morale during those long weeks when the workaday world grows dull and seemingly inescapable. The cabin gives you at least the prospect of "escape," whether or not you get away.

And don't forget—our economy could suddenly plunge us into a recession. A cabin could then become a haven of security for you until industry got under way again.

Thus, a cabin in some natural setting can become an important addition to what you have—no matter how much you have, and no matter what your occupation, business, or general mode of life.

If your search is for an economical cabin site, don't overlook the unimproved cabin. Read Chapter 6 in dealing with its unique advantages for unencumbered living. Its very simplicity and low cost hold an important key to low-budget living, and should be remembered when you consider location and type of site.

If, on the other hand, what you want is a commuter's cabin, which generally means modern in equipment, this calls for broader considerations. Transportation time to and from your work ought to be limited to an hour and a half each way, otherwise daily travel becomes tedious.

This one-room log cabin gains in design by the interesting stairway approach.

You should be able to reach the cabin in all kinds of weather. Beware of a site where you may be snowed in, and of summer roads that can mire a car or delivery truck after heavy rains.

You must think also of the other members of your family. If there is no social life for them, they will rise up in protest. The children must have access to a school. Other basic considerations for the commuter's cabin include such items as possible television reception, line connections to telephone and electric power, newspaper and mail delivery, to name only a few.

Within commuting distance of any large urban center, the waterfront site usually demands a premium price. A site with a good view that overlooks water or interesting scenery often comes into the same price bracket. Therefore, if you can find a way to get a road into some isolated site that by a miracle has been overlooked, you are very likely on the right track toward real economy and wise investment. If, for example, you can find the corner of a farm woodlot where the view has not been fully appreciated, and you can reach it by car, such a site offers great possibilities.

After years of experience in looking for sites, I am confident that many a golden opportunity still awaits the prospector. If your budget is close, take time to explore carefully the countryside near where you live. A tableland near a glen, a delightful hillside, a stretch of outcropping bedrock of no use to the farmer—these are rich possibilities for low-budget cabin sites. The chances are that most of these sites will be so densely obscured by trees or brush that no one but yourself will realize the valuable opportunities they hold.

But an even better and more direct method than personal search is to go to the county seat in the county where you want to build. Ask the county auditor for a list of tax-delinquent properties, and the descriptions and plats of each location. During your first free weekend, examine the sites. If you find something you like, pay the back taxes.

When the original owner has failed to pay the taxes for a certain number of years—in many states the period is five years—and you pay the back taxes, you can get what is called a "tax assignment" from the county. Your final ownership paper is about equivalent to a quitclaim deed. This is good enough while you personally own the site. Should you finally sell the property, it is best to have an attorney obtain a Torrens title for you, or procure a warranty deed through legal formality.

Cabin on the Yukon River at 50 Degrees Below Zero

A large number of such properties with unpaid taxes are available throughout the United States. If the original owner should pay up the taxes before the expiration of the five-year period, your tax money will be refunded to you by the county at an interest rate generally higher than most investments pay.

A point of caution: Do not pay the last year's taxes due until you have acquired a title from the county. These particular taxes cannot be refunded to you if the original owner redeems his property before expiration of the five-year period.

Cabin sites in the wilderness can also be had through the unpaid-tax method outlined. You will need some ability as a woodsman, however, if you are to find them. A wilderness guide can be of great help to you. He may find it an interesting change to be locating sites instead of hunting game. However, he may not have the knowledge for tracking down land descriptions and locating exact sites. Therefore, if you are hot on the trail of something good, you had better have the local surveyor first pinpoint your find.

It is not a good policy to build on a site unless it has been surveyed. An exception might be made where adjoining property has already been recently surveyed, or if some well established survey bearing is close enough to establish your own tract. But where a survey reference bearing marker is a long way off, the survey can become expensive, adding excessively to the cost of the land. Therefore, first get an estimate of the survey cost by consulting the local surveyor.

In some instances the federal government will lease sites in what is referred to as a "summer colony." Such sites, especially in a national forest area, are quickly becoming more and more limited.

In Canada, where it would seem that wild lands should be unlimited, rapidly narrowing restrictions are being enforced due to the heavy influx of American and other site seekers. Each province handles its own land distribution. Make your inquiry to the Department of Lands and Forests at the provincial Capitol. If the site is in the Yukon or Northwest Territories, make your application to the Department of Northern Affairs and Natural Resources, Ottawa, Ontario.

Sites in Canada can also be leased from the government at an annual fee of about $15, but in some provinces a substantial investment must be made in a cabin, whether the site is purchased or leased. This required cabin investment varies from $1,000 to approximately $2,000. Leases run from one to several years. Renewals usually are permitted at the expiration of these periods.

Several Canadian provinces are changing their entire cabin-site program because of surveying difficulties and other problems that confront the district forester when sites lie in isolated areas. The new plan under discussion is to establish subdivisions. Surveying will then be done by the provincial government. Lots will be numbered and roads built. All the applicant will be required to do is to select a site directly from a platted region, pay for it then and there, and build a cabin according to government specifications. This done—a patent on the site will be granted at once.

Islands up to 3 acres in area for private use, and up to 15 acres in area for commercial summer-camp use, can be bought in Canada at a cost of approximately $175 per acre plus surveying cost. Or if you prefer, such acreage can be leased at about $15 per year.

The United States Department of the Interior, Bureau of Land Management, Juneau, Alaska, reports: "Waterfront property under the jurisdiction of the Bureau of Land Management has become very scarce in the past few years and for various reasons. The major portion of Southeast Alaska lies within the confines of the Tongass

National Forest and no outright sales are featured by that agency."

A few tracts are to be auctioned off each year by the State of Alaska, where such tracts come into possession of the government from private individuals because of titles being given up for one reason or another. Purchase of privately owned sites offers greater possibility in Alaska.

Mexico is becoming increasingly popular for nonresidents seeking a mild winter climate. Sites can be purchased on application to the Secretary of Exterior Relations. Nonresidents cannot purchase sites within 100 kilometers of the Mexican border or within 50 kilometers of the Mexican coast. These precautions are for military, customs, and immigration reasons.

The choice of a site for a cabin to be used only seasonally to escape periods of severe temperatures, both hot and cold, poses a few factors not always apparent. You would hardly be wise, for example, to leave New York State or Minnesota, head south, and buy a site for a cabin in Arizona, New Mexico, or California to escape the winter's cold if such a site were at a high elevation. You might then leave a snow-storm in Minnesota only to land in a snowstorm in New Mexico. In the southwestern desert areas where the elevation is only a thousand feet or less above sea level, the temperature generally will be mild in January and February. But it must be realized that high elevations in these southwestern states experience cold winter weather during the same months as in the East or Midwest. Moving from hot to cool climates can usually be accomplished in mountain and desert states simply by going from lower to higher elevations in the same general region.

A similar mistake can be made by southerners in an effort to escape their summer's heat by buying a site in the northern lake region. It is just as possible in this instance to leave a temperature of 100 degrees in the South and arrive in a temperature of 100 degrees in the North during the summer. Generally, however, hot-weather periods in the North are short.

Do not be deceived, therefore, by tourist literature that shows the average high and low temperatures in a certain region. The average of high desert and low mountain temperatures can give a delightful 65 degrees, which is quite meaningless—or perhaps very meaningful of extreme temperatures at different elevations. When inquiring about temperature charts, ask for daily night-and-day reports of a specific area and elevation during the months when you plan to be in residence there. It might also be well to ask for reports of several years back, since there can be freak temperature years.

In selecting a desert site for mild-climate living in winter, the first question should be one of available water. The depth at which water may be reached by drilling can sometimes be learned by writing to the local government, or to a local well-drilling concern.

Lake region, mountain, or desert sites pose their own particular problems, in most instances depending upon the intended use of the cabin. For the remote cabin, perhaps, the best selection of a site is at the "jump-off" place; that is, at the very edge of the wilderness, or embarkation point. This will give you access to the wilderness on the one hand, and to the "outside" on the other. Such a site has proved a practicable, all-around living plan for a durable cabin location.

Where you want to spend some of your recreational time in the saddle, or where travel is to be by pack horse, and since you cannot very well own your own horses, choose your site near a cattle ranch where pack horses and outfits, or saddle horses, can be rented when you need them.

Choosing a site is not a routine job; it is an exploration of Nature's assets, but the search can be fascinating, and usually is, no matter where you decide to explore.

We must not overlook a very logical place to build a cabin—in our own back yard. This has become a popular concept in recent years. Where it is difficult, and in some instances impossible, to travel away from home, the back-yard cabin has offered an interesting substitute for wilderness living. In the penthouse we have a good variation of the same idea.

Where a lot is large enough, a cabin can be surrounded with a small grove of trees, evergreen or otherwise. And where still further adaptation is considered, a rock formation, perhaps with an artificial brook, can lend a simulated wilderness charm. If an air-conditioning unit is installed and if the cabin also has a fireplace, the joy of an open fire and a "cook-out" indoors in any weather are not beyond the compass of daily city life. In this way you can bring the wilderness to your own back door.

# 3

## Do It Yourself

THE FIRST QUESTION that occurs to the average individual when the problem of doing anything himself looms up is, "Can *I* do it?" My honest answer is that most people can. By nature we are creatures who can work with our hands and we can often produce surprising and satisfying results, satisfying to ourselves, and surprising to our families and friends.

It would not be unfair for the reader at this stage to say, "Prove it." Broad statements have a way of somehow appearing true if they appear in print, and for this reason I should like to offer some proof from my own personal experience that the do-it-yourself plan is a sound one.

The cabin in which I live for six months of the year, overlooking the Valley of the St. Croix River, an hour's drive from St. Paul and Minneapolis, is a successful do-it-yourself project, which I have called "One-Man House." Quarried stone and square timbers, pine paneling, plank flooring, a fireplace with a stone chimney are the main features of the cabin.

By word of mouth the cabin has found its way into press, radio, and television as a sort of showplace. All that I can offer in expiation is that in building it my experience with tools was that of a layman.

Apart from two rough wilderness cabins, it was the first that I built. Knowing my own limits, I can say in all sincerity that it could have been done by the average individual with only a household experience with tools.

If my accomplishment in "One-Man House" is still suspect, let me give the reader another example. When I entered one of the nation's organized youth camps more than a dozen years ago, to direct a wilderness program, the cabin in which I lived during my years of camp activity was built by 12- and 14-year-old boys under my direction. The cabin project was so successful as an activity that the camp manager agreed to allow the boys interested in cabin building to build a complete canoe base on the Canadian Boundary. The boys built two such canoe bases in the North in the years that followed.

Thoughtful medical men have a theory that you should have a project of some kind under way at all times. I have found it to be a valuable suggestion. Here in Canada's wilderness, in a 10′ × 12′ cabin that I finished a few weeks ago, I am writing this book every morning while I work every afternoon at building the main cabin. The trouble with this schedule is that when I am writing I want to be building, and when I am building I have the urge to write. Then, of course, there is always the lure of the trail. When I see a canoe gliding around the bend, I know that both building and writing are at a standstill for the day or longer.

But this is as it should be. Do-it-yourself projects should not be hurried. One cabin near "One-Man House" on the St. Croix River was built during weekends by a businessman from Minneapolis. I would see him at regular intervals transporting just enough lumber, on top of his car, to keep him busy over the weekend. This seemed like a leisurely way to build, and at the same time, I thought, very slow. Then came weekends when the roof of his car was empty of lumber as he passed my cabin. Thinking that he had lost interest and had given up the project, I met him on one such trip to ask, "How is the cabin coming?"

His answer was brief: "It's finished."

When you are building a cabin, it is difficult to realize the effect of time and steady effort. Two days of building during the roughing-in process will show great progress. The finishing-off moves slower. The roughing-in and roofing-in is the only stage when you need to work quickly. The only other operation to show faster progress than the

Demountable Concrete Form Used in Pouring the Foundation for "One-Man House"

roughing-in is the clearing of brush on the site. A few hours of work seem to perform a miracle.

Probably the most forbidding aspect of building your own cabin is the apparent, but not actual, size of the project when viewed as an individual undertaking. "How," a prospective builder asks, "do you go about mixing and pouring all the concrete foundation for a whole cabin by yourself? Why, the concrete would set up before you even got well under way!"

The answer is, "You don't."

The foundation for "One-Man House," the cabin on the St. Croix River, required 190,000 pounds of concrete for the foundation. If this seems a big job for one man, look at the illustrations of much simpler concrete forms in Chapter 9.

For the "One-Man House" the 190,000 pounds were poured in small sections, approximately 1'×2'×4' in size, during the weekends, over quite a period of time. I would often pour a section of cement, then go fishing, or take off for a jaunt in the woods to view the fall coloring along the river. When the spirit moved, I would pour several sections. The forms were quickly demountable, and could be used over and over again, until the foundation was completed.

Of course, this was a far greater undertaking than is required for an average cabin footing. Chapter 9 shows the method for making cabin footings where no basement is required—the more common way. Setting up forms and mixing and pouring concrete for simple footings are tasks well within the scope of the do-it-yourself cabin builder. Such footings can be done one at a time, or as many as time permits.

Where a cabin is to be built over an extended period of time, the exposure of a partly finished structure to the elements is a concern. That is why speed is essential in the roofing-in stage. I suggest that you rent a large canvas tarpaulin for covering the work. If there is no one available to help handle this heavy tarpaulin, plastic coverings may be used that will last just about the life of the project. These are easily handled, and inexpensive.

The reader who continues to doubt his ability to "do it himself" should think about the building of a cabin as a series of small, separate operations. In just the same way, when an automobile factory produces a car, remember that every individual part is produced by a separate department and that is how the car is finally assembled.

Similarly, when you build your cabin, take only one step at a time. Once the foundation footings are done, the laying of the sills and the floor joists (floor supports) will follow as naturally as breathing. These operations in detail and in order are discussed in Chapter 10, but I want to show briefly in this chapter that each successive step is self-contained and in no sense of the word complicated.

Once the sills and floor joists are placed on the foundation, the next and obvious step is to cover the floor joists with the rough subfloor, or underfloor. With the underfloor laid, you have a platform on which the studs (upright supports) for the walls will be raised. These studs, together with the bottom and top plates (horizontal connecting members), will be nailed together while you have them laid out on the floor, so that the whole stud wall section can be raised into position at one time. Four of these sections form the support for the walls of your cabin.

You will be nailing some, or all, of the board sheathing on the stud sections after they are up, to make them sufficiently rigid so that you can have good support for the roof rafters, or roof supports. Once the roof supports are up, the roof board covering will be nailed to them. If you now board or sheath the remaining uncovered part of the walls, you will have a roughly closed-in building, and you can then proceed to insert windows and doors, put on finishing siding, and complete the exterior.

Nowhere in this series of operations have you been involved in anything but the simplest kind of arithmetic and the sawing of plain pieces of lumber. If you like, you can put in the interior partitions later, and with no more difficulty than you had in the raising of the stud sections of the outside walls. If you follow the simple order shown in Chapter 10, you cannot go wrong.

This is a brief description of roughing-in a frame cabin built from lumber. The general sequence from footings to roof is not very different for a log cabin. The differences are shown in Chapter 9.

If I have one suggestion to make to you, it is this: "Don't hesitate to go ahead." If your lack of skill shows up in a few bad joints, the chances are a hundred to one that no one will ever notice them, and you yourself will forget them in time. This is borne out by the story of the telephone crew, busily working on a pole, slanting from a hole they had just dug. The irate lady of the house came running out, shouting, "For heaven's sake, don't put that ugly thing in front of my house!" The foreman in a few kindly words explained: "We're not putting it in, ma'm, we're taking it out. It's been here for twenty years."

Among builders it is an axiom that two men working together can do as much work as three working alone. In building a cabin there is a great deal of work for an "end man," one who simply holds the other end of something—a board, a tape, or a rafter. Here is where a friend or your wife can be mustered into service to great advantage. Even if your helper never drives a nail, he can be very useful as an "end man." But don't let him off that easy. Get two hammers, and even if your helper is a lady put one of them in her lily-white hands. It will pay dividends, and it will give her a definite personal satisfaction. I know ladies who can build as well as men; in fact, I know one whose occupation is laying cement blocks.

When I first began cutting quarried stone by hand, I found that as I progressed the results were turning out too smooth. My first efforts were rougher and better looking. Strangely, my inexperience helped. Some of the most attractive stonework that I have seen has been done by novices who worked with no skill but considerable art. Ignorance is a valuable factor in rustic stonework.

Be as individual as you like in building your cabin. The greatest danger is not so much your lack of experience as a tendency on your part to imitate standard methods, and accept conventional outside advice. If you have ideas of your own, original ideas which you wish to carry out, have courage and stick to them. It is good to attempt the unusual, despite what critics tell you. The chances are that they are jealous because you have had the courage to carry out a project different from or more ambitious than what they would attempt themselves.

It is a good plan to sketch out on paper every part of your work. No matter how poor an artist or draftsman you may be, the drawing will indicate the general proportions you need. This is valuable in determining the pitch of the roof or the eaves, door and window arrangements, and in showing the best proportions for the height and width of gable ends.

Building materials have undergone a vast change since I first began building my own cabins. Today every shortcut is being taken to package or factory-make the various parts of a cabin that once would have had to be cut by the individual builder from staple lumber and other materials. The first indication of this was the appearance of "4-square" lumber on the market. Wall studs were square at each end, cut in exact, uniform lengths, requiring no cutting or squaring before going into the wall. Now it is possible to buy all such building items "precut." These should not be confused with "prefabricated" materials.

The competition between firms selling "precut" materials and those selling staple lumber raises the question of whether the labor of precutting is not added to the price of staple lumber. This is denied by the factory on the grounds that the amount of waste lumber from a home built with staple lumber is far larger than if the lumber were cut scientifically in the first place. You get an example of this when you make a number of rafters with diagonal cuts. If the original pieces are carefully planned for length, it is possible to precut rafters and jack rafters with little or no waste at all. A carpenter planning his work and fitting these pieces on the job cannot possibly arrive at these short cuts to the same degree that precutting methods do. This is shown by the waste pieces around every job.

The do-it-yourself cabin builder should examine precut material, since it offers a valuable aid to the inexperienced builder. Because the various parts of the building are bundled and the pieces numbered, there is the added value of a building-erection method—an organized course of action.

Nowadays the packaging process does not stop with precut lumber. Chimneys are packaged in combinations of tile and concrete that make the building of a chimney very simple. Nevertheless, there are ways of putting your own ideas into play, and your own impress on the finished product. Packaged chimneys can be finished off around the sides and top with quarried stone, fieldstone, or brick. There is no necessity to follow slavishly the prefabricated assembly. The guide and support are there in the packaged chimney, to be covered with your own veneer of stone or brick.

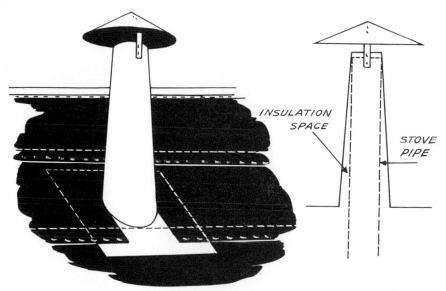

INSULATION SPACE

STOVE PIPE

Method of Flashing for Jack-Type Chimney, Showing Dead-Air or Insulation Space in Chimney to Prevent Condensation

Another development is the simple chimney, in a roof-jack type of metal and asbestos, easier to install than full chimneys, and now sold in packaged form. It is set on the roof, and simply nailed into place.

The accompanying illustration shows an even simpler type of chimney jack that provides a dead-air or insulation space between the pipe and the jack if it is properly made. Note how the jack tapers very abruptly from the roof to the cap opening when the stovepipe is inserted into the jack, creating a liberal dead-air space between the stovepipe and the chimney jack—an effective way of overcoming the problem of creosote condensing and running down your chimney.

Before you begin to build, look into these prepared items; then you can decide whether to buy them or to custom-make your own.

The problem of nailing down rafters at the plate or lower end has always been troublesome. Now a small, inexpensive stamped-out bracket holds the rafter by nailing the bracket to the top plates and the rafter. (See illustration.) Such nailing brackets also help in straightening and holding warped rafters erect. They can be had in a great variety of shapes and designs to meet various nailing requirements.

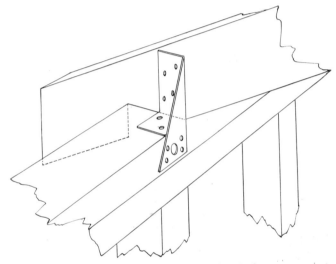

Top Plate Nailing Bracket for Rafters

One of the most convenient nailing applications is the use of fir plywood gussets (bonding plates) as shown in the illustration. These can be adapted to structural needs in any type of cabin, especially in creating roof spans, floor joist assemblies, and other points where a bond is needed between two members.

Finally, let me give you this piece of advice. No matter how much information you have acquired on materials, discuss your cabin with your building-materials dealer. Very likely you will learn from him some new idea or method that has lately come on the market to permit short cuts and better ways of doing the job. And if you are not certain about some aspect of your project, you will find your dealer almost always willing to help and anxious to please you.

Fir Plywood Gussets (Bonding Plates)

Have no fear that you will be alone in your venture. It should give you courage to know that other amateur builders will be tackling the same problems and difficulties as yourself. Today, and for a very good reason, do-it-yourself books are in great demand. As a nation we are rediscovering that intellectual exercise is not the only necessary part of a satisfying life. We are rediscovering that thought is an activity which occurs above and below the neckline. We are finding out that the body is a partner in the thinking process. Mental and manual exercise together shape happy lives.

Much of our thinking, we might say, is actually done with our hands. We can discuss an object with someone for an hour, but if we let him hold the object in his hands, his understanding of it will be immediately more comprehensive. In short, we need to get the physical feel of things—a factor that is frequently lost in a conventional education.

Besides, we cannot keep our health without bodily exercise. And bodily exercise, together with a strong interest in a project undertaken, gives balance to our mental and physical health.

One last suggestion. Before beginning the building of your cabin, make a scale model of your cabin-to-be. From an engineer, I learned that it is almost impossible at times to work out solutions on the drawing board. To see the problem best, he makes what he calls a mock-up, or module.

Your cabin model will be a priceless piece to set on the fireplace mantel someday. While you are working on your cabin, it will probably rest as a paperweight on the plans you drew. Chances are, you will be studying each part of the miniature oftener than you do your plans. Build the cabin mock-up on a scale of one-half inch to the foot. It makes an interesting rainy-day hobby that will pay off in many ways.

# 4

## Cabin in the Wilderness

IF YOU ARE planning to build your cabin in a wilderness area that can be reached by some kind of automobile road, your building problem is simple. In any wilderness cabin project the transport of materials to the site is perhaps the most important factor, certainly just as important as the cost of materials or of actual construction. But when you build on or close to a road you must bear in mind that if the area is convenient for you to reach by car, it is just as convenient for millions of others. True solitude under such circumstances is rarely possible, and your peace of mind will depend upon how much tolerance you can develop to tourist traffic.

However, to many people a cabin built where a car can be comfortably driven up to the door is all the wilderness required. The degree of solitude is for the individual builder to decide. In fact movement is not always from settlement to a more remote part of the world. One couple of my acquaintance gave up a beautiful secluded island cabin to live in an area densely settled by summer dwellers.

The effects of oncoming age and a preoccupation with their health have done much the same thing to many others. To be away from immediate medical help is a serious problem for the apprehensive middle-

This cabin, tucked into a rocky island of the great Cambrian Shield, looks out over a vast recreational wilderness.

aged, or even the young. But to a large majority the most disturbing question in cabin living is how much social life they require and demand. This matter of social life should be given careful thought. It can only be determined by actual experiment. In the last analysis, you may need more human contact than you think you do! Too many cabins in wilderness areas have been abandoned when their occupants discovered through living in them that solitude was something they wanted only in small doses. This is not the book, of course, to indulge in a study of human behavior patterns, but the question of solitude, how much or how little you can take, especially in this modern world, is far more important (and less easily resolved) than many of the questions asked on a psychiatrist's couch. If you find that you can depend strongly on yourself, and have both cultural and physical occupations that require or make living away from crowds desirable, the remote wilderness cabin, removed from auto or common carrier travel, is for you. If you have been dependent socially on others for most of your life and find that you are uncomfortable alone, then it is certainly unwise for you to build in the really remote wilderness places. Solitude then can become distressing, and on occasion tragic.

I know of one instance where the prospective builder of a wilderness cabin insisted that he must be at least beyond the first canoe portage, and by preference several portages beyond the railhead, in order to satisfy his desire for solitude. When he finally found the remote cabin which suited him and tried it out on a lend-lease basis, he spent so much time on the trail, visiting back and forth from the settlement, that when the lease was up, he had spent more days on the trail and visiting, than in the cabin. He is still a prospective builder.

How necessary to us is the company of others? I can only speak for myself. I think of myself as one of the lucky ones, one of the introverts. A great deal of my life has been spent happily in wilderness solitude. When in my youth I spent long periods alone in wilderness areas, there were occasions, nevertheless, when the rumble of the wind in the eaves of the cabin so exactly resembled a human voice or the sound of a canoe paddle, or the distant hoofbeats of a saddle horse, that I would go outdoors now and then to see if someone was coming, despite the fact that in the wilderness where I lived either horse or human being or canoe was almost an impossibility.

For those of us who are serious in wanting to be "away from it all" there is no easy solution. Moving into a more sparsely settled area is not the answer. The answer to our questions lies deeper than that.

If I were consulted, I would repeat what I have said earlier. Build your cabin at a so-called "jump-off" place or embarkation point. My latest cabin is so situated. Mail comes on the local train once a week, and that, I find, is often enough; it gives me a kind of weekly holiday, when supplies also come in. The train may bring a visitor or an Indian friend living back in the interior, about to embark on his journey by canoe to rejoin his people, perhaps after a visit at the Indian hospital. You may be sure no visitor will depart until I have warmed his spirit by food and talk. In other words, there is just enough contact with the outer world to keep me from loneliness, and not enough to spoil my pleasure in knowing that when I direct my gaze to the North from my cabin door, no mark of civilization breaks the line that extends to the North Pole and beyond.

If you are one of the populated areas' lost legion, as I am, one who must always push farther into the silent places, the "jump-off" cabin is not necessarily the end of the trail. Deep in the wilderness, remote even from the "jump-off" cabin, reached only by canoe, pack horse,

Cabin in the Wilderness

or dog team, will be rude cabins of a more primal crafting built of logs with the bark left on, a split-log floor, and a slab door. By building on a waterfront or on terrain where planes cannot land, you can escape the most ambitious effort to disturb your seclusion. Such cabins will generally be small, and roughly and quickly built. Like the Eskimo's igloo, they need not survive to the following summer.

There's a saying: "Give an Indian a pair of hinges, a few nails, a window sash and an ax, and he will fashion a cabin for himself in the wilderness." He has done it with far less.

No longer is there any need to transport fragile window sash over long distances on wilderness trails. Heavy transparent plastic of picture-window size can be rolled and easily carried. Half of the sheet serves for the inside window, half for the storm window.

Over the years I have built these primal cabins scattered a thousand miles or more over the wilderness. Since the logs used are of small diameter and the simple top-log notching method makes construction relatively easy, I have roughed up such cabins whenever work or research for any length of time, or even periodically, took me into some wilderness area.

The transportation of building materials to a wilderness cabin site can be a big task, costly enough on occasion to raise the question whether a cabin of lumber and other finished products may not be prohibitive. The problem is how to haul in flat-surface material, by which I mean floor and roofing boards, doors, and other items requiring planed surfaces to supplement the log construction or for the entire cabin if it is to be of frame construction. One solution to the problem is treated in a later chapter (page 86) where I discuss the use of a chain saw for creating dimensional materials and boards.

When such lumber is transported from the "outside," the important job usually is to get the material from a truck, train, or other common carrier to the waterfront level on which the cabin is to be located. It is often easier to unload at some distant point where the common-carrier line of transportation runs close to the water, and then transport the materials catamaran fashion across two canoes or boats to the site, using an outboard motor. (See illustration.)

When piling lumber across two canoes or boats, it is well to use two pieces of $2 \times 4$'s, or two poles, as guide supports in holding the two craft in the proper position for loading. Lash these supports to the gunwales with sash cord. Actually, the weight of the lumber will hold the two craft stable, but for the convenience on the empty

Canoe Catamaran with Lumber Cargo

return trip and for the first part of the loading, this type of assembly offers a simple operation. Always tie the supports so that the craft are about a foot closer together at the front support than at the rear support. This will keep water from splashing onto the load.

While an outboard motor may seem to be out of direct drive when installed on only one of the craft used in this combination, it will not be difficult to steer the load if the lake is reasonably calm. However, if you can set the motor on a bracket halfway between the two craft, the drive will naturally be more direct. Or two motors can be used—one on each craft. Paddles instead of outboard motors can be used if the distance is not great or if time is no object. Pile the lumber so that you have free paddling room at each of the sterns. If you decide to use paddles, utilize an improvised sail, whenever the wind is favorable.

If your lumber is to be flown in by plane, the plane load and the inside dimensions of the plane's cabin will have to be taken into consideration. On the average small plane eight-foot lengths are the longest dimensions permitted. Because a load of lumber on the undercarriage of a plane will change the entire aerodynamic principle of flight, most pilots will not risk this type of carry.

If your cabin is to be built deep in the wilderness, a chain saw can be an almost indispensable tool. Directions for its use begin on page 86. When you have learned how to use it, you can cut all your materials of the dimensional type, such as floor joists, rafters, and studs on the site. Then you need to fly in only the planed materials, like flooring, trim, and accessories. If you have no objection to rough-sawed lumber, even the floor and trim can be made with the chain saw.

As much as a thousand pounds of lumber at a time can be transported by canoe over water and carried over portages. Tie the lumber into portageable-size bundles, using binder twine at each end and the middle. Lumber, naturally, should be in as short lengths as possible for convenient handling. If the lumber must be transported in long lengths, three men can carry such material better than two, the addition of the third, or middle, man overcoming the troublesome up-and-down sway of the boards. In such portaging, the third man, being on the opposite side of the other two carriers, helps to keep the bundle from slipping off the shoulders of the two end carriers. All lumber lengths should be well planned for length to avoid needless carrying of waste.

Perhaps the best possible method for transporting large amounts of materials into the wilderness to mining-camp cabins and other projects is the so-called "Cat train" (Caterpillar train). Travel, of course, should be in winter across frozen lakes, rivers, bogs, and muskeg. There may be exceptions, as in my case, when I purchased an abandoned Indian school from the provincial government, dismantled the schoolhouse, and moved the materials by Caterpillar Tractor and pulp sled on open ground through a grown-over trail. Wherever the trail was somewhat hidden going in, it certainly was wide open coming out! The Cat ground all obstructions to pulp! Brought to the waterfront by Cat train, the materials were then transported on two canoes, catamaran fashion, as described, to the cabin site.

The vehicle called a "Snomobile," with eight rubber tires, a light canvas, rubber and stamped-steel caterpillar tread, with skis at the front-wheel positions, and with a large panel-truck body, is used a great deal in Canada, the United States, and other cold countries for transporting building material and backwoods' supplies. It will travel in snow without broken trails. It will carry about the same load as a one-ton truck, and can also pull a heavily laden sleigh-trailer.

A vehicle not beyond the budget of the average cabin builder is the motorized toboggan, which has come into popular use in recent years. It is about eight feet long and three feet wide, and has a two-cylinder motor that drives a small canvas and stamped-metal Caterpillar track. This toboggan does a good job through the snow, and will tow a toboggan-trailer. Its one shortcoming is that it can get fouled up in slushy snow. This condition, as a rule, can be avoided in most places. The outstanding feature of the vehicle is that, being narrow, it can be used over portage trails, if the trails are over terrain that is not too steep or precarious.

Over the desert, prairie, and other open country, even where no roads exist, the four-wheeled jeep-type truck can be used. Frequently in the desert you will run into terrain where the only transportation will be by pack horse, and this applies also to mountain regions where pack trails are the only routes of access, apart from the helicopter.

We must not overlook the use of the common truck in many roadless areas where we are prone to believe that trucks are not suitable. This applies, for example, to long hauls over frozen lakes and rivers. It applies also to hauls over open country if the ground is reasonably solid. When driving a truck over river ice, great care should be given to test the ice over the route. Just because a single test of ice shows ample thickness does not mean that such thickness prevails over the entire river. Currents can create risky places. Test the whole route carefully with a pole equipped with a steel spike at the end, and make deeper cuts with an ice chisel at all questionable points. If the snow is first removed over an ice-road route, the ice will freeze deeper in this exposed area.

If you have the real blood of adventure in your veins, you will somehow work out a way to get your materials to your chosen site. The natural barriers you encounter will discourage you if the wilderness life is not for you. It is only by such special effort that you can have the cabin you want—where each dawn breaking reveals some strange and impressive aspect of your hard-won solitude.

A wilderness cabin can be your first major adventure in living beyond your ordinary routine life. It will give you leisure and recreational living, but it will also become the basis for a greater understanding of the natural world around you. What we seek in Nature is not easily explainable. But through the wilderness cabin you can come closer to discovering the meaning and depth of your bond with Nature than by any other means.

# 5

## The Auxiliary Cabin

"CONFERRING HELP or aid, assisting, supporting; subsidiary, additional, serving to supplement," are some of the dictionary definitions of the word "auxiliary." And I cannot think of a word that better describes the most neglected cabin structure, one that requires the least possible investment, and is superior to the tent for the semipermanent camp. In fact, you might argue that the proper place to discuss the auxiliary cabin is in a book on camping, but its permanence, if permanence is desired, gives it importance in a book on cabins.

You will better understand its true value if you have lived in a tent for any length of time. If you are a camper you will realize that a 7'×10' tent is larger than the ordinary tent for two people. But when you apply these dimensions to a cabin, you are at once amused at its small size. This is because when we think of cabins we think in terms of spacious structures.

The 7'×10' auxiliary cabin can be prefabricated from waterproof plywood and light dimensional lumber, or it can be precut and assembled on the site. If it is to be made portable and moved from place to place over the years, it will, of course, have to be prefabricated into sections and bolted together when erected. If it is to be precut and assembled on the site, consideration will have to be given to the type of transportation to be used in moving it. It can be transported across two canoes, flown in by plane, or hauled in on dog sled or Snomobile. In pack-horse country it can be hauled in on a travois.

Of special appeal to the do-it-yourself enthusiast is the fact that the plywood auxiliary cabin can easily be built in a basement workshop during the winter months. Such working conditions offer an opportunity for leisurely craftsmanship and protection from the weather that make for good workmanship and ingenuity—rare virtues in the rapid outdoor type of construction.

The dimensions of 7′ wide by 10′ long have been so worked out as to give the simplest structure with the best possible arrangement. Upper and lower bunks at one end are suggested by the 7′-wide dimension. It is well to swing the top bunk downward on hinges against the wall. This gives head room when sitting on the lower bunk, and makes a perfectly satisfactory davenport—the upper bunk providing a back rest when folded against the wall.

The table will also be hinged, either supported by hinged brackets or by hinged legs. A folding chair or grub box will provide one seat at the table, while the lower bunk will provide the other.

Since the cabin is small, the stove should be placed as far from the bunks as possible, preferably under the front window to give the cook the benefit of direct light. Of course, when weather permits, most cooking and living will be done outdoors. A folding gasoline or butane camp stove should supplement the small wood stove during warm weather if cooking is not done over a campfire.

As many windows as possible should be used in a cabin of this kind, because windows give you a sense of being out-of-doors, and long spells of bad weather seem less confining when the scenic outlook is wide. It is well to set a small window into the wall at the head end of each bunk to provide light for reading while lying in the bunk; reading is apt to become a favorite rainy-day pastime.

Large louvers should be placed in both gables for full ventilation when the cabin is in use and for keeping it fresh and dry when unoccupied. Such louvers should be protected with insect screen, and then covered on the outside with heavy gravel screen to keep out squirrels. Hinged trap doors will be needed to cover the louvers on cold days when the stove is lit and heat is important.

The floor will consist of 3 sections, each $3\frac{1}{3}′ \times 7′$, made of $2 \times 4$'s

The 7' x 10' Auxiliary Cabin of Waterproof Plywood

and ⅜" plywood. Sill supports will be required under each side and center, the length of the cabin. This is not much of a problem in a wooded area, since 3 logs of small diameter slightly flattened on one side with an ax, and level on the ground, will do the job. If the cabin is erected on the desert or prairie, 4 × 4 sills should be provided. The 3 sections will be bolted together upside down with ⅜" × 4" wagon bolts and washers. The whole floor assembly will then be turned right-side up.

Sections for the walls work out best when vertical: 3 sections 3⅓' × 6' form each of the 2 long walls; and 2 sections 3½' × 6' form the short rear wall. The front wall will have only 1 section 3½' × 6', the door assembly replacing the other section.

Any arrangement of the windows, of course, must be made so that the entire window is included in one of the sections of the walls. Otherwise a window will span from one section to another and make assembly complicated. A cabin of this size should be kept simple. Plexiglas can be substituted for glass to prevent glass breakage.

On first thought, a flat roof would seem to be more economical in material and to eliminate the gable ends. The drawback of a flat roof is that your head is too close to the ceiling for comfort, especially during the hot summer months. Moreover, it adds nothing to the general appearance of the cabin. Of course, good proportions are not essential in a structure of this kind, because the overriding consider-ations are practical assembly and economy of material weight. The gable roof, however, not only gives a better-looking structure, but since much of the living in a cabin, while you are standing erect, is away from the walls, the gable-type roof permits more overhead room with lower ceiling height, and permits ventilating gables.

The roof will have 3 sections on each side, or 6 sections in all—each 3¾' × 3⅓'. This will give a "pitch" or roof rise of 1⅜' in 3½'.

There will be no eaves. The ends of the closed-in rafters, after being cut to angle, will rest on and extend only to the outer edge of the top plate. The rafters, of course, will be assembled as part of the roof sections, but will serve in the same manner as regular rafters, being cut at the ridge, and supported with a ridge board, to meet, at the correct angle, the alternate rafter sections on the other side of the roof. The roof plywood should be ⅜" stock, but ¼" or even ⅛" can be used for extreme light weight. Joists, studs, and rafters, attached to the sections, are not shown in the illustration (page 41) in order to give the reader a clearer view of the auxiliary cabin's section assembly.

Where the auxiliary cabin is built on the site, and not prefabricated, roll roofing, of course, would be used in the same manner as in covering any roof. But where the cabin is prefabricated and made to be portable and disassembled, a sheet of rubberized or nylon plastic material the size of the roof is first laid on as a waterproof seal. Then a waterproofed canvas tarpaulin, with loops or grommets spaced every few feet along the edge, is spread over the rubber or plastic covering. This canvas tarpaulin is then looped into screw hooks or eyes along the wall. Strange as it may seem, this laced rope is also used to hold down the roof sections. Nothing more is required, and you will find it adequate.

The walls, after being bolted together, are held to the floor sections by the same rope principle—although this is not shown in the illustration. Hooks along the floor sections, and another row of hooks along the lower part of the wall sections, are simply interlaced with No. 6 sash cord and drawn tight. The sections can also be bolted down, if desired.

The door-and-frame section is bolted to the other sections in assembly.

If the triangular gable sections are made with ⅜″ waterproof plywood, they need not be made into sections with dimensional lumber supports, but merely cut to size and inserted against wooden stop strips, and held in place with small latch bolts.

The wall sections are held together with bolts, nuts, and washers, which stiffen the entire structure. It is best to use wing nuts on all bolts, and tighten them only with the fingers. They will hold satisfactorily and will eliminate the need for a wrench.

## THE AUXILIARY LOG CABIN

The trapper, woodsman, or individual skilled with an ax will not bother to haul a plywood prefabricated cabin into the wilderness if the cabin is to be a semipermanent structure. Rather, he will build it of logs—but the quick way.

When I say "quick," I am assuming that the cabin will eventually be abandoned, after it has served its temporary purpose.

The auxiliary log cabin can, of course, have variations, from the temporary cabin built with unpeeled logs, a sheet of transparent plastic for a window, and a roll of tarpaper for the roof, to the more finished structure where the logs are peeled and plywood or lumber is transported for the roof and floor. If this sort of finished job is wanted, then you will follow the same general instructions for building the refined log cabin discussed in a later chapter (page 105). However, the quickly roughed-in auxiliary log cabin with unpeeled logs as a semipermanent camp is what we are concerned with here.

The logs will be cut to a diameter under 6 inches for easy handling. The proper underlog method of notching logs to avoid water traps and decay will be dispensed with, because the logs can then be quickly notched and the structure erected in a fraction of the time required for the finished underlog scribing and notching job.

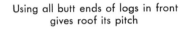

Using all butt ends of logs in front
gives roof its pitch

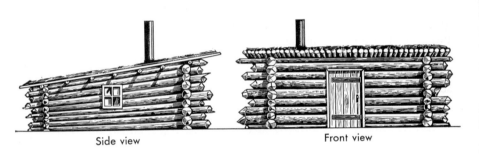

Side view                                        Front view

The Auxiliary Log Cabin of Unpeeled Logs—Semipermanent Camp

This fast method of notching is always a pleasant surprise to anyone who sees it done for the first time. It is a trick in campcraft that should be within the knowledge of all who travel extensively in the wilderness.

Begin by laying 2 parallel sill logs about 10″ in diameter down on the ground. Dig them into the ground deep enough to bury them halfway, and level them with the eye. Also, get them roughly parallel along the top side. If your cabin is to be 7′ × 10′, then your sills should be 12′, or over.

With an ax, cut 2 rough notches in each sill log, 10 feet apart. Cut them deep enough to receive about half the diameter of your end-wall cross-logs. Drop your cross-logs into these rough notches. Now cut 2 rough notches in each end log, 7 feet apart. Cut them deep enough to receive the side-wall logs, and drop these into place.

Repeat this same operation with the end-wall logs and the side-wall logs until you reach the top of your walls. There is no scribing or marking of corners, no parallel fitting of logs.

The impression most people get when they see this process is that it is something of a mathematical miracle. Invariably they are convinced that the operation will leave a half-log space between each log. This does not happen. Chopping halfway through each log as it is dropped into position is what accomplishes the so-called "miracle."

The whole process is very simple. Your rough notching will not matter. Even though all the notching has been done with an ax alone, and no gouge, you will be surprised how well the corners close up. Besides, you are going to chink any voids that show up with moss, and chink between the logs as well, so that your fit is not important.

Contrary to formal log-cabin building, do not alternate the narrow ends of the logs with the broader butts, which is usually done to keep the walls level. Instead, keep all butts of the side-wall logs at the front end. If the butts all come to the front you will see that when you get to the top of the wall, the front end of the cabin will be higher than the back end. This will give you a shed roof with the proper slant, which is what you want.

Now, lay slim poles side by side across the roof, and over these lay tarpaper or birch bark, held down with additional poles or dirt. Next, saw out spaces for your door and window, and frame up these openings with boards, if you have them. If not, use an ax and hew some pieces, as best you can, from split logs for the framing. These pieces can be narrow to avoid a big job of hewing. Nail these framing pieces into place, then hang your door and window. Of course, make your door of split half-logs—unless you have a few boards available or unless you are working with a chain saw.

You will see that this quickly built type of auxiliary log cabin is nothing more than a trapper's tilt. If you plan to stay in a region for some time, for hunting, fishing, or on a program of research, this is a valuable semipermanent shelter. It is also your first fulfillment of an ambition which I mentioned earlier, of a cabin deeper in the wilderness than your permanent "jump-off" cabin.

The auxiliary cabin, whether of frame or log construction, is almost a necessity when building a larger and permanent cabin in the wilderness. The frame type, because of its quick construction, gives an immediate foothold on the site. Perhaps, there is no problem in the building of a permanent cabin more frustrating than not to have adequate shelter during an extended construction period. A tent camp is one way out of this difficulty, but camping is a chore in itself, and makes the building job cumbersome. Also, if you are going to use help, your helpers may be reluctant to live in tents while on a job.

If the auxiliary cabin is to be a permanent complement to the main structure, it can easily be built on the spot from standard material. In this case, prefabrication is not necessary because your cabin can be erected so quickly that, for the short time involved, camping is not a problem.

Tent-Cabin with Frame Base

Obviously, the permanent auxiliary cabin should be conveniently placed to be of service to the main cabin. My experience has been that it should be placed not too far from the waterfront, as most outbuildings generally are. Because it will be a storage or cache cabin when the main cabin is finished, there is an advantage in having it near, so as not to have long carries to make to and from the waterfront. If you have sufficient frontage or area on your site, and the cache cabin is of good design, erect it off to one side and slightly back.

One of the most economical auxiliary cabins, more accurately called a "tent-cabin," can be made from a combination of wall-tent and a frame. This can be made from standard lumber. (See illustration.) A common type, logged up to a height of about 3 feet, forming a frame over which to support a wall-tent is also shown in the illustration below.

Wall-Tent Cabin Logged Up

The portable auxiliary cabin can be mounted, completely set up, on two canoes or boats, or on pontoons, as a houseboat, driven by an outboard motor. You can use this combination for living quarters while transporting your cabin long distances by water, ultimately to be set up on land. Such a craft, for example, if taken down the Mississippi, the St. Lawrence, or other rivers with locks, is allowed lock service. Before setting out, however, it would be well to consult the Maritime Commission for information on lighting fixtures, life-saving equipment, and other compulsory needs, regulations, and navigation etiquette.

Whenever I construct an auxiliary cabin, no matter whether of the portable or the temporary log type, I get the feeling once again, after the first tattoo of rain sounds on the roof, of "belonging" to the particular country in which I find myself. A few well stocked shelves with food and equipment, a stove, a simple board table, some empty root-beer cases for stools, a cot or bunk bed, a supply of books, and an all-band transistor radio suffice to make life complete, supply leisure, and offer the diversion that a fascinating country holds in store.

The auxiliary cabin reached a high state of perfection in the portable plywood form in recent activities of the United States government, and other governments, in Antarctica during the Geophysical Year. Hauled to almost inaccessible places by helicopter, these portable units have made life possible, and even comfortable, at the South Pole in temperatures that heretofore were encountered only at great risk.

The prefabricated cabin has gone afield. It holds high promise for almost every department of outdoor life, and serves admirably as a ski hut, an ice-fishing house, and the like.

# 6

## The One-Room Unimproved Cabin

In the long history of the cabin no more modern or elaborate type ever replaced, in the eyes of the real wilderness-dweller, the one-room cabin with limited improvements. This was the cabin of the pioneers. Despite today's insistence on "inside plumbing," the one-room unimproved cabin remains the ideal for most of us who value the solitude of forest and lake.

Furthermore, many of our complicated, high-maintenance improvements can be simply and adequately replaced or even bettered by the more primitive arrangements of the one-room unimproved cabin.

We have an excellent example of this throughout the Canadian Shield, which runs from the region of the St. Lawrence River, through some of our northern states, and on up to Alaska. In the Canadian Shield, where drainage systems have been installed for inside toilets and other drainage, an insufficient soil depth for the tile drainage run-off and for the use of septic tanks has created a grave health hazard. This has been especially noticeable in resorts where a number of cabins occupy a restricted area. The surface seepage in these drainage systems has become a pressing and unsolved problem.

In a discussion of the problem with a health officer, I was told that

49

The one-room unimproved log cabin is traditional in forest areas.

the most sanitary arrangement possible in country where rock is just under the surface is a properly constructed outside toilet, erected where a pocket of earth will allow for a sufficiently deep pit.

In today's world, the outside toilet is mentioned only in shocked whispers. With rare exceptions, almost every one of these structures is unpleasant. And yet the outside toilet can be a simply constructed unit, easy to build, and not only inoffensive but meeting every sanitary regulation.

Most health departments can furnish you with plans for properly constructed outside toilets. But these, even if you build them to required specifications, need refinements.

First, the pit opening must be covered with a concrete slab, except at the seat opening. The toilet seat and cover can be purchased from a plumbing house, but the toilet cover should fit tightly over the seat. A 10-inch opening, cross-ventilation channel, from the seat section to the outside, plus a ventilation-channel from the pit to the roof, screened at the openings, will be necessary. The outside structure must also be cross-ventilated with one screened opening near the floor and the other near the ceiling.

Here the rectangular log cabin has reached excellent proportions and quality in design. (Note uneven log ends.)

The common difficulty with most outside toilet structures is their cramped size, lack of light and ventilation, and the fact that their inside walls have a drab, unfinished board surface that cannot be kept bathroom-clean. To obviate this, finish off the interior with a coat of cheerful, washable enamel. On an enameled shelf or stand, always keep a pitcher of water, a washbasin, soap, paper towels, and an air-spray deodorant. Near the seat, keep a supply of lime in a metal container with a small scoop. Where ordinarily you would flush the toilet after each use, simply sprinkle a scoopful of lime into the pit. While the convenience of an inside toilet is not denied, even the overly fastidious cannot claim that the modern bathroom is always free from offense. And if the outside toilet were given as much cleaning care as the bathroom, there might be an additional point in favor of the outside toilet in that it is removed from the living quarters to the freely circulating outdoor air. Where the structure is properly located, something might also be said for a good view. (See Chapter 11 for outside-toilet gas wall heaters, controlled electrically from the cabin, for cold weather.)

Pour a solution of one package of yeast in one quart of warm, not hot, water into the toilet pit several times each season. The resulting fermentation will break down the deposit. Under no circum-

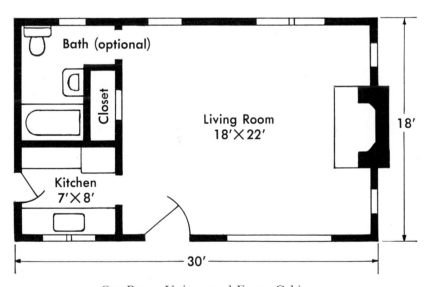

Bath (optional)

Closet

Living Room
18' X 22'

Kitchen
7' X 8'

18'

30'

One-Room Unimproved Frame Cabin

stance should garbage or other refuse be thrown into the outside toilet. This will set up a very disturbing form of putrefaction.

Garbage should be burned; and dishwater, along with other waste liquids, disposed of in a small, well-covered pit, dug a short distance from the cabin. Add a tablespoonful of chlorine (kitchen bleach powder or solution) to the dishwater just before emptying it into the pit.

Where no electricity is available, a bottle-gas refrigerator with a freezing compartment will take care of all summer-food preservation needs.

A washbasin and a bucket of water on a bench outdoors will take care of casual ablutions; and if the lake is too cold for bathing, the portable, galvanized bathtub is not impossible.

The kitchen corner of the cabin will have a combination bottle-gas and wood stove. (See Chapter 11 for a gas or oil auxiliary heating unit adapted to the kitchen wood stove.)

Portable gas-mantle lamps, of which there are many on the market now, will give as much light as a 100-candle-power electric light. If greater economy is desired, gasoline mantle lanterns giving equally good light, or Aladdin mantle lamps, can be substituted for the gas-mantle units. Butane gas from large cylinders can be piped to wall and ceiling mantle lighting fixtures. An electric power plant is a possibility, but the noise of the gasoline motor makes it a nuisance where wilderness solitude is desired.

To maintain your health, you should exercise sufficiently every day to induce active perspiration. If every possible convenience is at your elbow your opportunities for natural exercise are much curtailed. For this reason alone, the physical activity required to maintain your unimproved cabin should not be regarded as a disadvantage. Carrying water from a spring or lake can furnish the exercise you need to maintain a healthy body.

One reason why the one-room cabin with no modern improvements other than the incidentals mentioned continues to retain its nostalgic hold is because its simple construction makes it easy for almost anyone to build. It is the almost perfect do-it-yourself operation. And even where the cost entails hired help, or contracting for the construction, it is not beyond the budget of most prospective cabin seekers.

Whether your one-room cabin is to be made of logs, frame, or

Stove

Single Room
10' × 12'

3' × 7'
Bunk

3' × 7'
Bunk

4' × 10'
Sheltered Porch

Metal-
lined
box

Folding
table

One-Room Unimproved Log Cabin with Protective Overhang Roof

stone, the best and most traditional design, I have found, is first to give good proportions to the gable end, and then to make sure that the rectangular proportions of the cabin are long enough so that it does not look too square. It is difficult for me to get away from the design shown in the illustration where the roof continues out in front beyond the main structure in a liberal protective overhang. I spend much time in my doorway when a heavy rain is falling, and the protection of the overhang is delightful.

In a wilderness cabin there is always a need to set or hang things outside. My canoe paddles go up under the extended roof, and there are hooks where I can hang a pot of stew to cool, out of reach of pets, sled dogs, or forest creatures. It is not unusual to come upon a cabin of this protective roof style and see snowshoes, packsacks, saddles, and other gear hanging up. These are the items that give a wilderness flavor to a cabin. Under such a roof firewood can be stacked against the wall where it will be fully protected from the elements.

A screened porch on the front of the cabin is not a satisfactory substitute for this type of roof extension. If you want a screened porch, build it at the back or on the sides. No view was ever improved by a fuzzy mesh of screen and its obstructing frames. From the front of the cabin you should be able to see an unobstructed panorama, where the eye can move from whitecap to racing cloud, from valley to mountain peak framed only by the great trees in the foreground.

Even under clear skies, when no roof is needed, an overhang will act as an eyeshade for a view of the opposite shore, to identify the occupant of a canoe coming down the lake, or a rider on his mount, moving along a mountain trail.

Your overhang should be complemented by a low porch platform the full length of the overhang. The edge of the platform makes an ideal spot to sit with your feet on the ground. It seems the most natural place to serve a pot of tea or coffee, when alone or with a visitor. It obviates the need of porch furniture. Your coffee cup is right at your elbow.

Actually, no railing is needed on such a porch, but I think a railing lends a certain charm. It should be substantial enough to sit on, to accommodate those of your visitors who prefer a rail to a chair. Packsacks, saddles, and other items will naturally be flung over it to dry or for convenience' sake. And if your cabin is in the cattle country, it will make an excellent hitching rail for saddle horses.

This type of cabin lends itself well to log, frame, or stone construction.

As indicated earlier, frame cabin building materials should have a rugged appearance. For a frame cabin, the best wall covering I have found is lap siding of rough, unplaned boards. Lumberyards now stock such rough boards for siding, but in order to get uniform thickness they are apt to plane one side. The rough side, not the planed side, is exposed. The only advantage of an even thickness in boards is a good fit when such boards are abutted end-to-end along the wall. But by planing, the thickness of the siding is lost and also its rugged aspect, which is its original quality and charm.

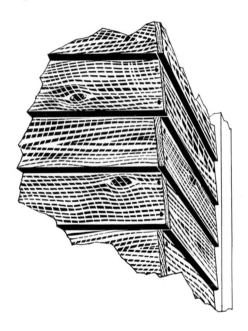

Rough Board Lap Siding for
Rugged Frame Cabin

There are two ways of using the unplaned boards as lap siding and gaining the advantage of their additional thickness. One is to select enough long boards to span the entire wall above and below the windows, and thus avoid all or as many joints as possible for butting. Long boards are not always available, although boards 22 feet long can sometimes be had in regular stock. The other method is to shim under the thinnest board so that it will be forced out even on the surface with the thicker board to which it is abutted. Personally, in order to preserve their original ruggedness, I prefer to shim rather than plane down the uneven thickness of the boards. Where the wall has windows and doors, shorter lengths can be used, and thus no end-to-end butting is necessary if the lumber lengths are properly planned to reach from the corners to these openings. (See the illustration of board siding made with a chain saw on page 88.)

Lumber companies have been made aware of the demand for a rough-surface board lap siding. As a result, you can now buy a rugged, standard-sawed wide lap siding with rough and smooth surfaces, called "rustic siding." As in the narrower and thinner lap siding, commonly used on city dwellings, one edge is thin, the other thick. However, in the rustic siding mentioned, the thick edge is over an inch, while the width is 10 inches. This gives an effective shadow relief to the wall and a rugged appearance to the cabin in general. The rough, sawed surface, not the planed surface, is exposed here also.

The rustic siding is nailed to the studs in the same manner as common lap siding. As implied, it is lapped—usually about 2 inches. Unfortunately, any lap siding does not go directly on the studs without leaving voids through which insects and air can enter the cabin. The cabin needs to be sheathed before applying this type of siding. If greater economy is necessary, and only a single layer is to go on the wall, then the cabin should be sided with a wide drop siding. This is a tongue-and-groove type of siding, common in all lumberyards, that has a cutout on the surface to give it a shadow relief—a rather shallow one, however, and not as attractive in its general effect. It makes a tight wall, and can be covered with a rougher type of siding later, if desired.

A very rugged type of siding that actually creates a wall without stud supports is made from heavy 3" × 5" ornamental tongue-and-groove planks, set vertically. A molding edge is provided, cut into the planks to give it a finished effect. It is expensive but not exorbitant when you consider that the planks provide both outside and inside finished surfaces, and need no stud supports.

Another type of siding featured by lumber yards today is made from rough-sawed boards with untrimmed edges. There are two types— where the bark is removed and where the bark is left on. In either type you have a board siding that has rippled edges, conforming to the uneven shape of the log. It creates a very effective rustic wall. I suggest, however, that the bark be removed from the logs before sawing the boards. If this is not done, the loosening bark will in time give a "shaggy mane" appearance to the wall. The surface of the boards is not planed, or should not be, so that a rustic effect may be obtained.

If your lumberyard does not have this type of siding, you can buy logs, peel them, and have them sawed into siding at a local sawmill. The siding should then be stacked with air spaces between them, and dried, or kiln dried for speed.

Here is an exceptionally good opportunity to create this type of siding with the chain saw. Once the boards have been sawed with the chain saw, and dried, they are ready for the wall, since no planing or edging of the boards is required.

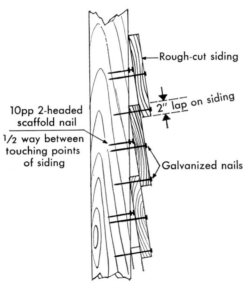

Method of Nailing Rough Board Siding

Rough board siding, such as described, usually is lapped about 2 inches. In the above cross-section illustration, you will observe that a void is created under and along the full length of each board, owing to this lapping, which has no contact support. This was an objection to rough board siding because it had a tendency to warp into the void and check-crack the siding.

This problem is overcome by using the type of two-headed nail illustrated—a nail sometimes used for scaffolding where a nail requires a protruding head for convenient pulling. The nail is driven into the stud under the siding, down to the first head, so that the unsupported central part of the siding rests against the protruding or end nailhead for support. A galvanized rustproof common nail is then driven through the siding from the outside, and together the two nails grip the middle part of the siding.

This inner-outer grip method of nailing has proved very satisfactory and has made heavy board siding an excellent and economical cabin material.

Where siding from two walls meets at the corners, lap the ends of the siding alternately at each course for best effect. See the illustration on page 56.

The use of rough boards for siding is probably most noteworthy in what is termed "board-and-batten." It is especially common in Scandinavian countries. Perhaps its greatest structural advantage is that, being put on the wall vertically, it lends great support, serving much the same function as studs in a cabin with horizontal siding.

Most simply described, this siding consists of plain boards, rough or planed as suits the owner, nailed vertically on the wall. The parallel joints of the boards are then covered with wooden strips. While a simple strip of wood nailed across the joint of common boards is the usual method of construction, a better way is to have the lumberyard mill out shiplap edges on one side of the boards and also on the battens. This allows the batten to be inletted or inserted in the two grooves of the shiplapped edges. This not only laps the joints but gives a staggered seal against rain and wind.

Various patented types of batten siding are available, some providing an ornamental batten molding, but where rough boards are used, this ornamental batten seems out of place.

Board-and-batten siding can be blind nailed; that is, nailed so that the heads are concealed. The difficulty here is that the center of the board, which must be wide for good effect, gets no nailing support. If you blind nail this siding, I suggest that you also put nails in the center of the board. These nails, of course, should be galvanized to prevent rust-run.

In Chapter 10, "Building the Frame Cabin," the extensive use of siding-cut plywood surfaces is described. This material, in combination with other sidings already mentioned, holds great possibilities in cabin design.

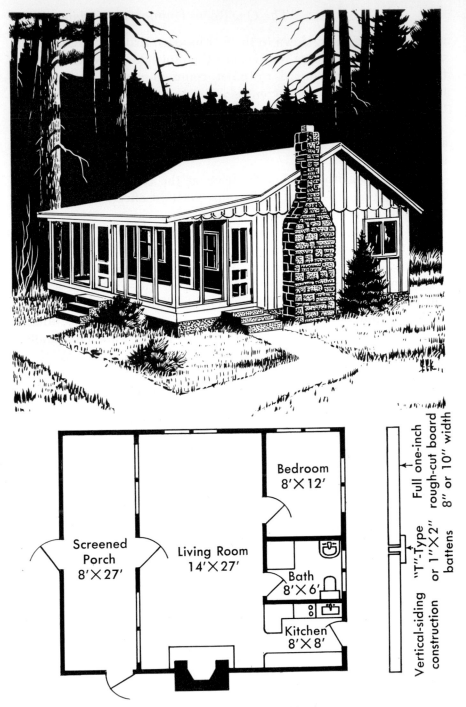

Bedroom
8'×12'

Screened
Porch
8'×27'

Living Room
14'×27'

Bath
8'×6'

Kitchen
8'×8'

Full one-inch
rough-cut board
8" or 10" width

"T"-Type
or 1"×2"
battens

Vertical-siding
construction

"Board-and-Batten" Cabin

When 4 × 6 timber rafters are used and placed farther apart than 16 inches from center to center of rafter, these heavy rafters give a rugged, attractive effect. Actually, doubly-strong 4 × 6 timbers spaced 32 inches apart are no higher in cost than 2 × 6 rafters spaced 16 inches part.

In spacing timber rafters 32 inches apart, instead of using the usual shiplap for roof boards, an additional strength advantage can be had with tongue-and-groove 6-inch flooring, V-jointed, or with plywood, for the 32-inch span. This finished material then, with no further effort, provides an inside paneling to set off the timbered ceiling effect. After this paneling is laid, 2 × 4 stock is nailed flat on the roof over each rafter position. Insulation then is placed between the 2 × 4's, and the entire roof sheathed with shiplap—finally, with whatever roofing is to be used.

Where the cabin is made of logs, the one-room rectangular design simplifies construction. A common school of thought in cabin building

An Economical and Unique Adaptation of Vertical Logs, Faced on the Interior with Lumber

advocates cutting out for windows and doors after the logs have been laid up. This type of construction has no serious drawbacks, and perhaps some advantages, particularly where transportation is no problem and long uniform logs are readily available. Amateur log-cabin builders, however, will find full-length logs difficult to handle, and if some of the logs can be used short, the problems of transportation and the cost of the logs are reduced.

When shorter logs are used, they should be cut slightly longer than necessary where they extend into the window and door openings, then sawed off later on a vertically drawn line. It is obvious that these log ends, where they project into the window and door openings, will have to be held in place as the log construction goes up. A temporary board brace nailed alongside the log ends will suffice. In Chapter 9 you will find a method for spiking these log ends, but the board brace should be used despite the spiking, in order to keep the inside logs plumb as the wall goes up.

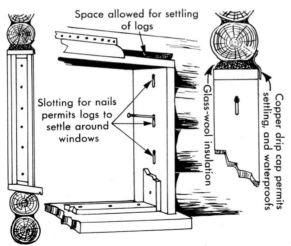

Method of Slotting and Spiking Window
and Door Frames for Log Cabins

The purpose of spiking is that when the building settles through log shrinkage, the spike slides in a void to compensate for the thickness of the dried logs, allowing them to come together. Spiking of log to log is sometimes left out in small cabins. However, it has the advantage in a cabin of fine workmanship and large size of preventing logs from springing out of place as the building dries and settles.

Window and door frames should be installed in a manner regarded as "floating." That is, they must not be spiked to the logs in such fashion as to allow the logs, when drying out and shrinking, to settle their weight on the spikes.

To accomplish this, I slot the door and window frames about 2 inches vertically at a position where every spike is driven through the door or window frames into the log ends. As the logs settle, the head end of the spike slides along these slots in the frames. As far as appearance is concerned there is no objection to this slotting because the door- and window-jamb strips cover these slotted areas. (See illustration.)

The common method of allowing for log settling and for securing window frames is to put a spline on the window frame and then notch out the ends of the logs to receive the spline. It is a big job, and I find it quite unnecessary. The above method is much simpler, and will be found perfectly satisfactory.

As I have indicated earlier, and as is shown in the illustration, a space or void must be left in the log immediately over the windows and doors to allow the logs to settle without throwing their weight on the frames. About 2 inches will be sufficient space above a window and 3 inches above a door. This is average, and much will depend on the logs, whether well seasoned or green. It is well to nail a strip of sheet copper as a visor over these voids to prevent rain leakage. Nail only the upper edge of the copper visor, as shown in the illustration; then it will adjust to the log shrinkage.

The general theory to keep in mind in the construction of log cabins is that all logs should be supported by the logs below them. None of this ponderous log weight should rest on window, door, or louver frames.

Rafters for log cabins need to be round—peeled poles from the forest. The tendency in recent years has been to use commercial square timber or plank rafters in log cabins. To my mind this has an unnatural and disturbing effect. Conversely, in a frame cabin all stock should be square to be complementary. On the other hand, I think it is impractical in a log cabin to use round poles and hew them flat for floor joists, where such joists are buried out of sight under the floor. This seems wasted labor. In remote wilderness areas where the transportation of commercial square floor joists would overbalance all other considerations, hewing out floor joists from round poles for flat nailing surfaces, of course, is labor well spent. Where the chain-saw method is used to cut floor joists from poles, no real problem exists in either situation.

Squared-timber porch posts generally conflict with logs in appearance. I made the mistake once of putting round peeled collar beams inside a frame cabin. They seemed so out of place, that I eventually removed them and put in square timbers. Conversely, square timbers would have been just as disturbing to me in a log cabin.

# 7

## Modern Frame and Log Cabins

THE WORD "PACKAGED" has entered our modern vocabulary to describe any complete factory-made building-unit formerly built by hand in part or entirely on the job. The most common reason for using these packaged items is the high cost of labor in hand-built units. The reason for not using them is the loss of individuality and exclusiveness in cabin design.

Today there seems to be a trend less toward the highly individual than toward the merely presentable, or at least toward the popularly attractive. You want a good-looking car, and the fact that there are millions like it does not take from you the pride of ownership. There might even be a desire, as with a good car, to conform—living and building very much as others do. This is not to say that there is not a wide individual choice in the packaged units available to you. But whether you are a do-it-yourself enthusiast or hire your builder, the use of packaged units will not greatly alter your basic building procedure. In other words, you will accept a certain standardization and live happily with your choice. If you feel about your cabin as you do about your car, the fact that there are thousands like it will

The log cabin can be imposing and modern.

not affect your pride of ownership, provided that your cabin, like your car, conforms to your standard of acceptance.

On the other hand, if you possess an individuality which demands that it be expressed in log or stone, you will not be satisfied with less than your own individual creation. You are the do-it-yourself enthusiast to whom this book is primarily addressed. Whatever your course, let me suggest that the cabin you have built yourself, by your own labor, following your own design, will have a distinction and originality that no custom-built structure can match, at least in your own eyes. Nevertheless, there are certain advantages in the use of packaged units and conventional assemblies. To take only one example, demountable panels in doors and windows in packaged assemblies allow for quick, easy change from screens to window sash, and when you close the cabin an additional wooden panel can be inserted, fastened on the inside, for safety against prowlers.

Whatever you decide, when your cabin is built, it should represent the achievement of a purpose, the fulfillment of an ideal.

**Air Conditioning** The most practical unit for cabins is the refrigerating type, although if you have a good supply of spring water you might do well to investigate water-cooled units. There are various types and special adaptations in all of these units—one feature being the actual washing of the air in the room by its passage through cooled water. Combinations of heating and cooling from one central control are available also, a thermostat keeping your cabin at a selected temperature the year round.

For information on heating units, see Chapter 11.

**Water Supply**    If the cabin is in an area where a well can be drilled, you will probably not have to worry about the water supply. The well must be deeply drilled to make certain surface water is not being tapped. If the well is shallow, the water should be tested, not once but at regular intervals. Where water is taken from a spring, tests should also be made for assurance that spring water, and not surface seepage, is being obtained. If you are fortunate enough to have a good spring at a higher elevation than your water tap, it can be piped into the cabin with no more than gravity feed.

If the water supply is to be taken from a lake, river, or stream, the water should be tested for purity. As a rule, a chlorinating plant is almost a necessity, but where the cabin is in the wilderness, and the direction of flow is from the wilderness, there seems to be very little chance of contamination. The water supply, for cooler temperature and clearness, is best pumped through a pipe extended along the bottom of the lake to a distance of a hundred feet or more from shore. To keep out sand, gravel, and vegetable matter, a filter point should be attached to the pipe at the source. Information and illustrations regarding pressure tanks, pumping units, and chlorinating plants for your particular application can be obtained from your local plumbing-supply house.

**Sewage Disposal**    Simple sewage disposal for the unimproved cabin has been covered in Chapter 6. Equipment for the modern cabin involves grease traps, septic tanks, and dry wells, or tile drainage fields. (See illustration on page 68.)

If you are on the rocky Shield that runs through the region in the United States from the St. Lawrence River to Alaska, and you find only a shallow layer of soil on the surface, needless to say you are in trouble for drainage. The sewage from your drain tile will come to the surface, wash into the nearest body of water, and endanger your health. If such a bedrock condition exists, I suggest that you see Chapter 6 for details of an outside toilet. Inside chemical toilets that may be emptied daily into the outside toilet are available from plumbing or mail-order houses.

If you are in a region where the ground will allow absorption, you can of course install the conventional bathroom with all its accompanying facilities. The sewage passes into a septic tank. These are numerous in design, materials, and capacity, and are generally made of concrete blocks, solid concrete, or steel. After the drainage from the cabin enters the tank, it stands and ferments. Through fermentation the solids break down into liquid. The liquid spills over into what is called a "dry well," or into a branch system of near-the-surface

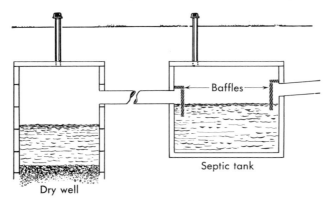

Baffles

Septic tank

Dry well

drainage tile. This tile allows the liquid to seep into the ground. There is also some surface evaporation, but no objectionable odor is created because of the high earth filtration process. Kitchen sink drains usually enter a grease trap before running off into the septic tank, because grease can block fermentation in the septic tank. Such grease traps are readily cleaned, and should be, at frequent intervals. The proper size of tanks and adaptation to special soil conditions can be obtained from your local plumbing-supply house.

**Lighting and Power Equipment**    Under the Rural Electrification Administration (REA) in the United States, electric power has now been extended into many hitherto inaccessible rural and wilderness areas. Where current is not yet available, the alternative is a private power plant.

Battery systems allow storage of excess current from the gasoline generator, or from a wind generator mounted on a tower. The battery system is the most economical because it allows any desired amount of current to be used. Where current comes directly from the generator, the normal or full capacity of the generator is used. For this reason the generator should be kept just large enough to equal the load.

Plants come in various voltages: 6, 12, 32, and 110. For lighting only, the 6- and 12-volt units will be found perfectly satisfactory. Since we are discussing modern cabins, where cooking stoves and other appliances are to be used, a 110-volt unit is almost essential, since most standard appliances are 110-volt units. The battery system is relatively less with the 32-volt system, but where current comes directly from the generator 110-volt systems are more satisfactory. See Chapter 6 for auxiliary types of lighting equipment.

I should mention at this point that electric wiring in log cabins entails a problem of concealing the wiring to outlets, different from that practiced in frame cabins. If you are to have an electrician wire the cabin, show him your plans before you begin construction so that he can provide channels between logs, under doorframes, or wherever outlets call for special concealment of connecting wires. If you are a real do-it-yourself builder, intent on doing even your own wiring, it would be well in any case to have an electrician check all your work to ensure that you have not created a fire hazard. In fact you may find yourself involved in a legal technicality by doing the wiring yourself. Certain states call for licensed wiring before the power line is allowed to be hooked up to a cabin.

**Foundations and Footings** These are often made too shallow. If a basement or cellar is not to be included, column footings of poured concrete or concrete blocks are ample, and perfectly satisfactory. Footings of any kind should extend below the frost line to prevent the cabin from heaving out of shape. In some parts of the North, footings can be set shallow on bedrock. Where a cellar is to form part of the cabin, or where there is to be a full basement, the cellar or basement walls are best constructed of concrete blocks; or forms can be built and the walls poured with concrete. Methods for constructing footings, cellars, and basements are described in detail in Chapters 9 and 10.

**Sills and Floor Joists** These should rest directly on the foundation and support the whole cabin. Here it is unwise to practice economy. I have seen floor joists made of such small-dimensional material as 2 × 4's. Sagging, creaky floors will invariably result. In all the cabins I have built for myself, I have used 2 × 10's, and I would not even consider floor joists less than 2 × 8. It may be argued that short spans require smaller-dimensional stock, but because short spans call for additional footings and a center sill there is really no economy.

**Subfloors**    The surfacing lumber under the regular floor can be made of common boards, shiplap, or of plywood. Shiplap is common board lumber, with a slight lap milled into the edges. This eliminates open cracks, adding somewhat, by tight sealing, to insulation. Plywood as flooring can be laid rapidly, and where the floor is to be of tile, linoleum, or other special cemented-on covering, the subfloor should be plywood. When shiplap is used for subflooring, it must be laid diagonally. As will be apparent, when the top floor is laid lengthwise over the diagonal shiplap, the top floor will cross the subfloor at an angle no matter in which direction the top floor is laid. This direction will vary according to the length of the room.

**Studs**    The upright wall supports of the cabin are generally made of 2 × 4's. If these supports can be of clear fir, they will be strong and at the same time economical. It is important that they be straight.

**Top and Bottom Plates**    These are the dimensional stock rails, generally 2 × 4's, to which the studs are nailed. They will have to be straight and long. If they can be extended the full length and the full width of the cabin, the walls will not have to be weakened by splicing the plates.

**Rafters**    The dimensional roof supports are usually 2 × 6's. These should be of clear fir, and straight. Any slight curve in a rafter should have the arc up. The weight of the roof will then have a tendency to bend it down and straighten it.

**Roof Boards**    The underroof covering or sheathing is generally of shiplap, but to speed up the job ¾-inch plywood can be used.

**Wallboards**    Underwall covering or sheathing has generally been of shiplap, until recent years when a great many pressed boards and also plywood have been used. The advantage of pressed board for wall covering is that it is soft and porous, and thus has considerable insulating value. Its strength is inferior to shiplap or plywood. If you prefer strength to insulation, sufficient insulation can be packed into the walls between the studs. In country where there are heavy winds and storms, which is almost everywhere, building strength is important and lends a feeling of security. Shiplap put on the walls diagonally offers tremendous support, although some waste is encountered in the angle cuts at the corners. Plywood, making a rigid wall, is a tighter seal than shiplap. It is a very strong and satisfactory

Cover either the flue tile or the packaged chimney with stone for best effect.

sheathing, and because it comes in large sheets it is quickly applied.

**Siding**   The outside wall covering is greatly varied in design and materials. I have already indicated the rugged and cabin-like appearance of unplaned boards for a lap siding. The choice continues to be wide, heavy commercial siding, heavy shingles, dressed-and-matched molding boards laid in crisscross mosaic patterns, log siding, board-and-batten, and today many commercial products simulating the above in aluminum and pressed materials. If I may repeat my earlier suggestion, avoid using any siding that is not wide and rugged in appearance.

**Chimneys**   Being both practically and artistically functional, chimneys should be selected for their effective architectural appearance. They come variously packaged, with full instructions for installation. The chimney built on the job, and constructed of stone and brick, will at once seem to offer the best design; but we must not overlook the fact that packaged chimneys can be used for a base, and by the addition of natural stone and brick can be made to appear hand built. This is accomplished by installing the packaged unit and then covering the exterior with brick or stone. When stone or brick is to be used on the outside, this fact must be taken into consideration when buying the chimney, because what are known as corbels must be supplied to support the stone at the base of the chimney where it extends from the roof. If the exterior is to be covered with stone or brick, the packaged chimney will usually be larger below the roof line and smaller above the roof. This difference is then made up by the building materials. Or actual corbels (projections from the face of the packaged chimney) are provided at the roof line for the stone or brick to rest on. (For a steel roof-jack chimney, see Chapter 11 and also the illustration on page 27.)

From my own point of view, no chimney was ever too large. Low-pitched roofs and large chimneys are a combination that always seem to be good design. Quarried stone gives a better effect than cobblestones. If you decide to use cobblestones, it is better to break the cobblestones with a sledge and set them in place, with the flat face outward.

Flashing the
Stone Chimney

**Porches, Terraces, Recessed Approaches**   These and other breaks in the uniformity of walls and roofs often lend a charm to the cabin that would otherwise appear too solid. However, avoid too many such breaks, for they can create a "gingerbread" appearance that destroys the best effect. Porches should never have the appearance of having been tacked on as additions. Rather, they should be built in, and appear to be an integral part of the whole.

When you build an enclosed porch across the front of a cabin, remember that you are blocking off the front façade of the cabin, as well as the light and view. Unless porches can be made so as to avoid these disadvantages, it is wise to have screen porches at the back or sides built into the floor plan of the cabin. Most often a front porch appears best at a corner, but it can form the central third of the long side of the cabin with equal effectiveness. Porches can be glassed in or enclosed with jalousies to provide an extra room for use in both cold and warm weather.

**Eaves**    Though eaves are often overlooked, they are vitally important in the general design. One-story cabins with relatively low walls lend themselves well to wide eaves as protection to walls and windows from rain and sun. While architectural pattern will be important in determining the width of the eaves, your judgment must be adapted to location and climate. Where the sun beats down at high temperatures and shade is a valuable asset, it is wise to keep the sun from the walls and windows. On the other hand, in an area where every ray of sunshine is welcome, shade is unnecessary and wide eaves can be dispensed with. In fact in extremely cold countries wide eaves can often cause roof-leakage. Roofs warmed by heated interiors melt the snow; the water runs to the eaves, where it freezes, and there builds up an ice block that prevents runoff. Then the water backs up on the roof, causing leaks. This problem is most severe where shingles are used. There is, of course, a way of roofing under the shingles, near the eaves, that will allow water to stand in such areas in pools without getting through the roof. A wide flashing of aluminum, tin, copper, or even a sheet of roofing under the shingles will prevent leaks but will not eliminate the ice. The ice should be cut away at intervals, or if you can afford it a section of the eaves can be supplied with electric heating elements which melt the ice and allow the water to run off. These luxuries can be procured on special estimate from your electrician.

**Interiors**    Interiors in cabin design offer a broad and infinitely varied prospect, as well as a decorative problem more challenging by far to the imagination than the ordinary home. Let me make a first general suggestion. Consider the possibility of at least one wall whose normal-dimensional 2 × 4 studdings are to be increased to a depth of from 2 × 6 up to 2 × 16. You will see at once that this in-the-wall space will have many uses: clothes closets, general storage space, recessed bookshelves, gun and fishing-tackle cabinets. The kitchen should also be considered for this wide-stud, deep-wall construction. The advantage of storage for food, dishes, pots and pans, built-in refrigeration, freezer, and dishwasher suggests but a few of many uses of the in-the-wall principle.

Portions of this deep-wall area in kitchen, bedroom, and living room will be finished off with panel doors in some instances, while others

"Deep-Wall" Construction for Recessed Bookshelves, Cabinets, and So On

will be open cabinets. Open cabinets make interesting display areas for guns and attractive dish and pottery showpieces, and allow space for exhibits where the wilderness theme may be accented in the general interior scheme. Large areas of such walls can, of course, be blind doors, camouflaged to appear as straight wall paneling.

While it is common practice to space studs 16 inches apart from center to center for strength, it is obvious that the spacing of 2″ × 16″ studs for cabinet space can be random, for varying cabinet sizes, because of the superior strength of such wide studs. The strength here in 2 × 6's to 2 × 16's is so great as to more than compensate for narrower spacing with the common 2 × 4's. The proportions of the various cabinets can be taken into consideration as the studs are spaced in the wall.

Radios, television sets, air conditioners, wall furnaces, hi-fi and stereophonic equipment, fans, folding beds, folding desks and tables, wall safes—all these can be accommodated in deep wall-space areas. Streamlining and absence of clutter make for easy housekeeping.

Another highly adaptable aspect of deep-wall construction allows the roughing-in of the cabin for occupancy, leaving the cabinetwork for a fascinating rainy-day hobby, where your imagination can expand ideas at will and in leisure.

**Fireplaces**   Structural methods for fireplaces that do not smoke are given technical treatment in Chapter 11. I mention fireplaces here for architectural reasons. Often they are delightfully imposing structures that form an entire end of a room. If the wall is well planned generally, such design becomes attractive and practical. But when the wall space around the fireplace seems to be lost and "floating" in the pattern, the fireplace can detract from the general appearance.

Fireplaces ought to be so constructed that the open front can be screened off entirely, allowing the fire to burn out at night unattended; otherwise the furnace heat in the cabin will escape up the chimney.

Heating units, circulating room air, can be built into fireplaces or left out, depending on whether or not increased heat from the fireplace is required. They greatly aid do-it-yourself fireplace construction.

Franklin stoves and other such units, like fireplaces in appearance and cheer, are charming as well as satisfactory. Besides, they are much easier on the budget. Such units can often be set up on complementary bases of masonry or brick, with designed wall-tile backgrounds, so as to lend color and charm to a room, and dignify the fireplace stove.

If fireplace stoves are piped for butane gas, a simple, quickly removable burner of the gas cooking-range type can be inserted for a steady night fire, and as quickly lifted out in the morning so that wood may be burned again. Manufacturers make fireplace stoves of many varieties, so that your choice of design and size is broad. Heating and hardware firms carry this listing. (See Chapter 11, "Fireplaces and Other Heating Units.")

**Ceilings**   These need more structural attention and artistic treatment in a cabin than is generally practiced in conventional dwellings. I get a feeling of roominess from the open underroof ceiling that is refreshing and cheerful. Some sort of timbering effect should be considered; otherwise the area becomes monotonous. Timbered effects are not pleasing unless the timbers are of fairly large size, 4 × 6 being a good choice. The paneling that shows between the timbers is best put on top of the timbers when the roof is laid; otherwise it involves fitting the paneling between the timbers.

If the conventional 2 × 6 rafters are used, and if the paneling for the ceiling is nailed under and covering the rafters, it is well to break up the large flat-appearing areas with collar beams, spaced to balance the ceiling. Support pieces, running fanwise from the center of the

Ceilings need more structural attention.

collar beams to the roof, give support to the roof and lend much to the general appearance. Where such beauty can be combined with utility, there appears what I like to call a reasoned beauty, or structural propriety.

Well insulated, well ventilated high ceilings are cool in summer; low, well insulated ceilings warm in winter. The latter, of course, are easier and more economical to heat. Louvers placed in the gables of open underroof ceilings greatly assist in ventilation and are conducive to low room temperatures in summer.

**Furniture** Conventional, deeply upholstered design is inappropriate in a wilderness cabin interior. Just as the deep wall suggested in this chapter conceals many of the desirable gadgets that make life easier and more entertaining, it is possible to utilize comfortable natural-wood couches, chairs, and other conventional units so that they will be in keeping with the cabin environment.

Though heads and horns of game, mounted fish, animal pelts, and so on, are common in hunting and fishing cabins, it is doubtful that stuffed animal heads thrusting from a wall do more than clutter what might otherwise be an attractive cabin interior. Perhaps a den, partitioned off from the main cabin, may be decorated with such items, but trophies, in general, are in bad taste.

76

Structural members can add much toward attractive interiors.

**Log Cabins** Cabins of the modern type are not so far removed from the general theme of wilderness frame cabins as to need special treatment of each phase. However, here too we want to create exteriors and interiors in keeping with the wilderness. Strangely, we have greater difficulty in furnishing a log cabin than we have in furnishing the frame structure. The basic problem lies in the fact that we use elemental forms to build a log cabin in the wilderness, and

77

Bunks are in keeping with cabin interiors and structure.

then utilize mass-produced products to furnish the cabin interior.

Despite the conflict between primitive materials and modern industrialization, the log cabin persists as a durable and effective architectural design. Its chief attraction is that it lends itself so well to a wilderness area, or even to the developed region with an informal landscape. Even when logs are not available, we try to gain the same effect with wide so-called "log siding." (See illustration on page 80.)

The modernization of a log cabin entails difficulties. Much of the plumbing that could be placed in the walls of a frame cabin can be concealed beneath the floor in a log cabin. As with electric wiring, if plumbing is to be concealed provision must be made at the time plans are drawn to allow for cutouts for such installation, and these must be made as the logs are laid up. Obviously, this involves expensive labor, and where the installation can be made under the floor, under door and window frames, under the outer layer of roof boards, in closets and other concealed places, to do so is simply good economy. If the log cabin is to be used in winter, concealed plumbing must be installed where cabin heat will prevent freezing.

**Log Cabin Interiors** Such interiors lend themselves better to furnishings made from natural materials than do those of frame cabins. Diamond willow and driftwood made into furniture can be used but should not be overdone. Furniture made from a combination of natural woods and rawhide, such as you see in the construction of snow-shoes, is very effective in log cabins. The manufacturers of such furniture supply some excellent designs in chairs, rockers, and other novel pieces that have the virtue of permanence. What is more, you learn

A More Formal Treatment of Logs on Lake Superior's Forested North Shore

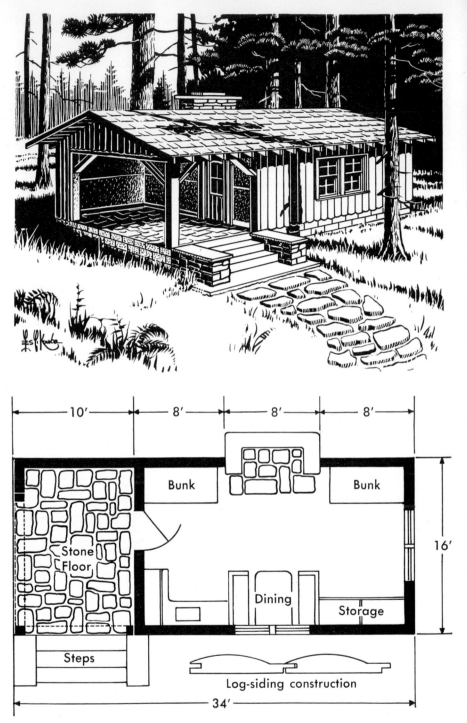

The Log-Siding Cabin

to value them as you would a fine piece of period furniture or a treasured antique. Their biggest attraction is that they never fail to "belong" in a log or frame cabin.

Lacing rawhide into natural wood frames can be a do-it-yourself project. Buy green calf or cow hides from a packing house or meat market. Soak the hides in a solution of weak lye or wood ashes for a day or two, until the hair slips. Remove the hair with a dull scraper while the hides are draped over a log. Wash the hides thoroughly —a number of soakings will be necessary—and then stretch them on a wall and allow them to dry. Now cut the hides into strips about a quarter of an inch wide, and soak them again, this time allowing them to dry only long enough so that they still feel damp. Then you are ready to lace them into your frames. As the strips dry, they will shrink until the lacing is as tight as a drumhead. As soon as the lacings have become thoroughly dry, give them several applications of spar varnish, and they should take on a translucent amber color that results in a most pleasing effect in complement with any natural wood frame.

Commercial easy-chair cushions of leather built into natural wood frames lend themselves well to both frame and log wilderness-cabin interiors. While offering the comfort desired, they do not give the incompatible formal appearance that plush fabric upholstery imparts. Leather has the natural sheen of autumn leaves, and gives a mellow touch to natural woods, rawhide furniture, and other wilderness materials.

Do not overlook the value of interesting colored maps for wall decorations. Framed in natural wood, without glass, and given several coats of clear, flat varnish, they take on an antique appearance that sets off any natural wood wall.

A V-jointed plank floor with dowels, or any natural wood floor of wide widths, is most in keeping with the wilderness frame or log cabin. The doweled floor can be screwed down and the screw holes filled with dowels—but I hope you will do this the "honest" way. Bore holes through the floor into the floor joists. Dip the dowel stick into waterproof glue, then drive it into the hole, and roughly saw off the dowel to floor level. When you sand the floor, the dowels can be leveled and given a crafted appearance that will be a complement to your construction.

The cabin of stone and timber is not often seen, but certainly it is no more of an accomplishment than undertaking to build a log cabin

The combination of stone and timber creates a rugged cabin.

of the finished type, or even a frame cabin of substantial custom-made materials. For some strange reason, the amateur builder has a tendency to shy away from concrete work, or the laying of stone, brick, or even cement blocks. He generally regards the mixing of mortar and concrete as a complex physical process beyond his powers, which it certainly is not.

Nowadays mortar comes already mixed in dry form, requiring only the addition of water to form the proper mudlike consistency. Concrete is a simple matter of combining 1 part of Portland cement, 3 parts of sharp sand, and 5 parts of clean gravel, boulders, or crushed rock, with enough water to make a thick mixture, but not too heavy to pour into forms.

Stone, brick, and cement blocks are laid up with mortar as masonry. Concrete is poured into wood, metal, or commercial paper forms, allowed to set for a day or more, and then when the concrete has hardened the forms are removed.

**Cement Block Cabins**  In warm and tropical regions the adobe cabin is of traditional importance. While these cabins can be made, and still are being made, from mud-brick, tamped dirt, and other primitive methods, the simulated "adobe" cabin made from concrete blocks falls within the compass of a chapter in which we are considering modern cabin materials. Because a concrete block is hollow,

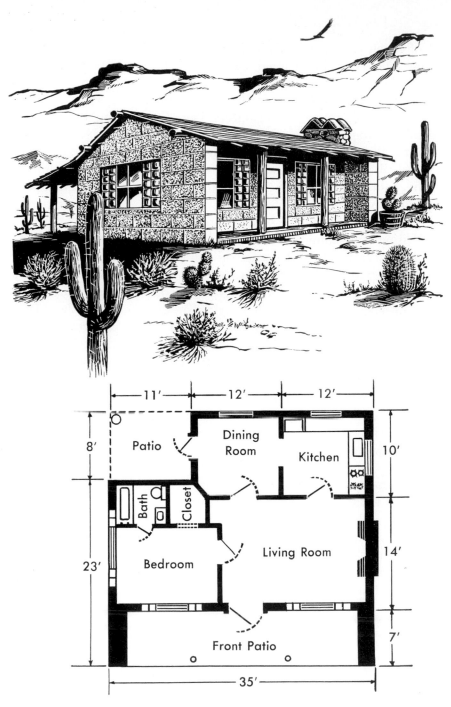

Simulated "Adobe" Cabin of Concrete-Block
and Glass-Block Construction

83

it offers an excellent dead-air space for insulation. The space within these blocks can also be filled with a new type easy-to-pour insulation.

A cabin of this type that has great appeal is one built from concrete and glass blocks with a cement-paint splash finish, white tile roof, and protruding round timber rafters. Here we are using the log-cabin theme of round rafters. Perhaps for traditional reasons, the round rafter is the one that looks best in the simulated adobe cabin.

Red tile conducts heat, and preferably should be painted white, or some light color, to reflect the heat of the sun. The cement-paint splash finish on cement-block walls, in a variety of colors, imparts a very rich note to this type of structure.

Wiring and plumbing in cement-block cabins should be installed as the blocks are laid, otherwise you will encounter the same problem of hiding wires and pipes as in log-cabin construction. Though the hollow cement blocks permit concealment of pipes and wires, where cement-block cabins are built in cold regions water pipes should not be laid through the hollow blocks because such pipes would freeze. Here, insulation and interior finish are needed.

In warm climates where there is little or no frozen ground to consider, deep footings are not necessary. However, a good wide concrete footing below ground level should be poured before laying up the cement blocks. Also, the soil under such footings should be well tamped with a timber to ensure uniform settling of the walls.

Window and door frames are set into place as the blocks are laid.

Baked commercial tile roofs are heavy, and require substantial rafters, closely spaced, for adequate support. In warm areas such cabins are often left with the cement-block surfaces exposed on the interiors. Variously colored cement paints can be used for these interiors—generally a flat finish in pastel shades. In cold climates interiors of cement-block cabins should be insulated and finished off.

If interiors are to be finished off in wood paneling, cement-block walls must first be provided with wooden strips to which the paneling can be nailed. Various methods are used for attaching the strips to cement-block walls, one of the best being the use of metal straps set into the mortar joints, and providing a hole in the side of the strip for nailing. Bolts can also be used, with the head embedded in the mortar; the strips are then bolted on. Nuts must be countersunk below the strip surface. If additional insulation is desired, it can be placed between the strips behind the interior paneling.

There are a great many interesting ideas to be incorporated into cement-block cabins, one especially being the use of glass blocks and decorative tile masoned into the walls. Glass blocks can be set flush with inside wall surfaces or with outside wall surfaces. When set toward the inside, an interesting window-relief recess and sill are provided on the outside. When the glass blocks are kept to the outside wall surfaces, an illuminated recess is provided on the inside where plants, books, pottery, and various decorative items can be placed, greatly enhanced in beauty by daylight illumination.

Where cabins are made from quarried stone, such stone can be procured either with sawed uniform mortar surfaces or rough from the quarry—but it must then be cut with stone tools.

The principles of construction used for cement-block cabins can be employed in stone cabins. Where cobblestones are used, either with round surfaces or broken with a sledge and with the flat surfaces placed outward, they are laid up with concrete in a form and allowed to set for several hours—but not for more than a day. The forms are then removed, the surface mortar scraped off with a piece of shingle, the cobblestone surfaces wire-brushed, sponged with water to clean the stone, and then, a day or two later, washed with a mild solution of acid or vinegar and water to neutralize any remaining lime deposit. A good drenching rain or additional wash-off of the stone will give the final touch to the surface.

# 8

## The Chain Saw and Other Tools

THE CHAIN SAW is a new concept for the woodsman. For the pioneers the greatest handicap to building a log cabin deep in the interior wilderness was the lack of tools easily and rapidly to create flat material for floors, roofs, doors, and windows.

Now a woodsman can load his canoe, pack horse, dog sled, Snomobile, or plane with the equivalent of a lumberyard simply by adding a chain saw and a supply of gasoline to his equipment.

Not many of us can remember the whipsaw. It was the only tool our ancestors had with which to create boards from saw logs. A platform was built on which the log was raised for sawing. One man stood below the platform, while another stood on top of the platform, and laboriously, with each man at work on his end of the saw, they sawed the length of the log to create a board. Whipsawing went out as the sawmills came in.

Today the chain saw is the rapid whipsaw. One man rips off board after board in a fraction of the time it took two men on a whipsaw. (See illustration on page 88.) By attaching a steel guide to your chain saw and running the blade along one of the surfaces of the log, you can saw a board. Planks, boards, or timbers can be sawed from the entire

86

The trapper's cabin is wholly hand wrought from the forest.

log simply by repeating this operation. The chain saw is a portable saw-mill.

When sawing boards, planks, and any other flat stock from logs with a chain saw, lay out the cut on the small end of the log and cut off the slabs on four sides to straighten the log, which is heavier on one end than on the other. The next cuts will be uniform boards from end to end. (See illustrations on pages 88 and 89.)

Though the ability to saw boards, planks, and timbers with flat surfaces on all sides is an important attribute of the chain saw, creating single flat surfaces on round poles and logs is perhaps the greatest advantage of this saw when one is building a cabin.

By laying two poles or logs together on skids or sawhorses, holding the logs together with log dogs, and running the chain-saw blade between them, two flat surfaces are created at one time, each log acting as a guide for the other. The value of this operation is immediately apparent. You now have floor joists, rafters, and studs from the forest, on which commercial lumber can be nailed to create straight walls, floors, and roofs.

Another important function of the chain saw is logging up. Sawing down a tree (felling) has always been an awkward task even for two men because of the horizontal angle of the cut. The chain saw makes this relatively easy, since keeping the saw in the cut is all that is required. Most limbing of felled trees, and the cutting of logs into proper lengths, are now also done with the chain saw.

In frame-cabin construction we discover another advantage of the

Creating Boards with the Chain Saw

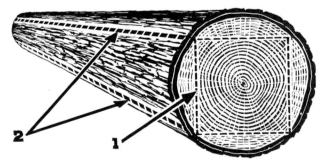

Lay out the cut on the small end of the log.

Cut off the slabs on four sides.

chain saw: use of the rugged materials mentioned earlier. Such materials give us what the artist calls "broad drawing." While this has been possible through purchase of planks, timbers, rough-sawed siding, and other rugged materials from lumberyards, we now can create these items with a chain saw—material picturesque beyond anything we might ordinarily be able to get commercially. (See illustration of cutting stair plates, boards, planks, and other items on page 90.)

The first effort toward refinement of the log cabin, as we have

Creating Two Flat Surfaces on Logs or Poles at One Time with the Chain Saw

Creating Stair Plates, Boards, and Planks with the Chain Saw

seen, was the squaring of timbers. Owing to the accepted beauty of round logs, it is debatable whether we can call this a refinement. But round-log construction was, nevertheless, considered by the early pioneer merely as something to be tolerated until a frame house could be built. In those days squaring of timbers with a broad-ax or adz, because of the broad fit in the joints, created a warmer cabin than one made of round logs, and gave the added advantage of smooth walls inside. Such walls were a housewife's domestic claim to distinction.

Squared-timber cabin construction might have a possible resurgence now that the chain saw has made the creation of squared timbers from logs a relatively simple and practical operation for a cabin builder. The broad, parallel fit in the joints between squared timbers gives this type of construction added appeal. However, the chain saw now makes it possible to create broad, parallel fit in the joints of round logs.

The tendency among some log-cabin builders is to run the chain-saw blade between the logs as they lie in the wall to remove the

The Semistockade Log Cabin

unevenness and close up the joints. Theoretically, this seems feasible. In practice, you run into trouble with the notching operation.

A better way is to lay the logs to be fitted on sawhorses and clip the logs together with two iron log dogs so that the logs won't roll or separate. Then run the blade of the chain saw between the full length of the logs. If the logs still do not close up well, bring the logs together, reset the log dogs, and again run the saw blade between the logs. *Logs must be fitted by this chain-saw process top and bottom, full length, before the corner notching is done.*

The chain saw has very much come into its own in the stockade type of log cabin; that is, logs placed vertically in a wall. This type of construction has not been so popular because horizontal logs seem traditionally more picturesque, and lend an interesting effect when extended beyond the cabin corners—an effect lost in the stockade principle. What the stockade type of cabin needs, perhaps, is a little more architectural consideration, since effective stockade cabins have been built. (See illustration.)

An advantage of the chain saw in making the stockade cabin is that

the vertical logs can now be made to fit snugly by the simple process
of running the chain-saw blade down between the log edges before
the logs are set vertically into the wall. This cuts out all irregularities,
allowing the parallel edges to meet.

Half-log construction, another aspect of the stockade type of cabin,
has its most important feature in the overlap principle involved, pro-
ducing a very tight wall. These are logs ripped down the center from
end to end with a chain saw. As the illustration will show, the flat
surface of each half-log covers the joint of two facing half-logs, thus
tightly closing up the joint between them. In short, the outside half-
logs are staggered with the inside half-logs.

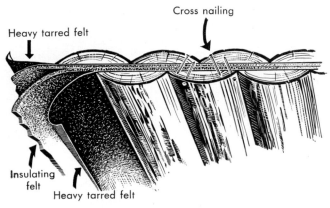

Heavy tarred felt

Cross nailing

Insulating
felt

Heavy tarred felt

Half-Log Stockade Principle

The general appearance, both inside and outside, is that full, round
logs, such as are seen in the regular stockade type of cabin, are being
used. The big advantage, of course, is that insulation and waterproof
paper, or roofing, can be applied between the two layers of half-logs,
whereas the full round-log cabin needs chinking or other between-log
sealing.

Another valuable aspect of the half-round stockade type of cabin is
that a flat wall surface can be created on the interior by using only
a single course of half-round logs. This not only saves in room space
because of the flush interior construction but also greatly simplifies
application of paneling or other wall finishes.

Paneling in this type of construction is nailed horizontally, directly
on the flat side of the half-logs, thus bonding them together. In using
this method of finishing off the interior, plain roll roofing for water-

proofing and insulating felt should be placed between the half-logs and the paneling.

Where paneling is to be applied vertically, the flat surface of the half-logs should be stripped with 2 × 4's, laid flat. However, this interior flat surface of the half-round logs should first be covered with roll roofing to seal out moisture. After the 2 × 4 stripping has been applied over the roofing, insulation is inserted in the spaces between the 2 × 4's, and the paneling is then nailed vertically to the flat side of the 2 × 4's.

Whether you use full-round or half-round construction, the logs in the stockade cabin are simply spiked, top and bottom, into plank plates. No notching of any kind is required.

When the advantage of the chain saw in the construction of the half-log cabin is better known, there is bound to be an upsurge in the direction of this type of cabin. The do-it-yourself builder will see at once that the handling of half-logs in the stockade type of cabin is a far simpler task for him than wrestling with long logs of the larger diameter used in the horizontal-log cabin. Also, he will realize that much shorter lengths can be used—a point in favor in transportation. Then, too, the taper of short-length logs is unimportant where the joining edges are trued up with the chain saw. Moreover, short logs are usually more readily available.

In addition to the vertical half-log construction, the chain saw has made possible the horizontal half-log cabin.

Logs for the horizontal half-log cabin are halved with the chain saw and edged in the same manner described for the half-log stockade type of cabin except, of course, that the half-log sections, running the length of the cabin, will be longer.

The illustration on page 94 shows an exploded drawing of half-logs notched very much as the round logs are notched, using a saddle type of notch, but, of course, fitting half-logs instead of full round logs.

This type of cabin, not generally well known, produces a flat wall on the inside, a log effect on the outside. Finishing off the interior with insulation and paneling becomes relatively easy. Perhaps the one objection to this type of half-log construction is that the log ends that extend beyond the outside corners are only half-round. Sections of the half-logs can, of course, be coped and fitted into these half-log ends, but this is a big job. However, the effect with the half-log corners is not objectionable.

The horizontal half-log construction that seems to have the greatest appeal is the one that permits a log effect both on the exterior and interior. Here the inside course of half-logs is staggered and lapped at the joints with the outside course of half-logs, giving a very tight wall.

In this type of construction, door and window frames are made from 3-inch planks created with the chain saw. We are not concerned in this type of log construction with half-log shrinkage and settling as with the use of round logs.

In the half-log stockade type of cabin, we can indulge our bent for insulation between the inner and outer half-logs to any extent we desire.

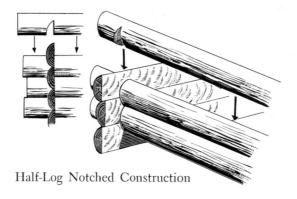

Half-Log Notched Construction

The half-logs are held in place by spiking into the ends of the half-logs, through window and door frames, and through "V" plank corners. Spiking the outer half-log to the inner half-log is also advisable for best structural results. Galvanized spikes should be used to prevent rust-run stains on the logs. One hazard that will occur to the reader is that water might get in between the outer half-logs and the insulation. To avoid this, the joints on the outside half-logs should be calked with compound, using a calking gun. Also, a lightweight roofing should go between the insulation material and the outside half-logs. One of the best points in favor of half-log construction is that logs sawed in half give up moisture with much less risk of checking.

By writing to chain-saw manufacturers you can obtain free booklets that will show in lavish detail the proper methods under all conditions for felling and sawing logs to proper length. The chain-saw manufacturers have done much research for their free booklets on the use of the chain saw, and not to avail yourself of this valuable information before using a chain saw would be folly. Safety measures also are well covered in these booklets.

The investment in a chain saw is not limited to cabin building alone. Clearing the site, cutting firewood and other general uses make the chain saw almost an indispensable asset to wilderness living. Your neighbors will want to borrow it; and since the chain saw has a running life like your car, your lending discretion will be based on your generosity.

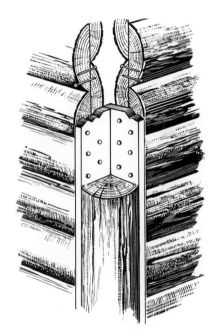

The V-Plank Corner

## OTHER TOOLS

**Lug hooks** are used for carrying logs.

**A cant hook** is used for handling logs on land. It is similar to a peavey but does not have the screwlike spike at the end.

**A peavey** is similar in some respects to a cant hook, but it has a screwlike spike in the end for handling floating logs on timber drives.

**Log dogs** are iron rods, bent at right angles near the end and

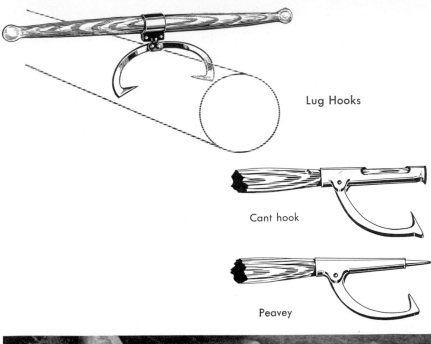

Lug Hooks

Cant hook

Peavey

Log Dogs for Holding Logs

sharpened to a point, used for holding logs in place while working on them.

**Augers** and **gimlets** are used for boring holes in logs. Gimlets actually are small augers.

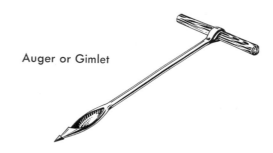

Auger or Gimlet

**Adz** The blade of an adz is set at right angles to that of an ax, but unlike an ax it has a beveled edge. It somewhat resembles a grub hoe. When the edge has been ground straight across (straight-faced), the adz is used for hewing flat surfaces. When the edge has been ground with a curve (lip-faced), the adz is sometimes used for the cuplike corner-notching operation of logs, and for cutting the channel-like groove that allows one log to fit parallel and snugly against another log.

**Axes** come in various styles and patterns. The double-bitted ax is used more frequently in log work than the single-bit, although here personal preference rules. The double-bitted ax has two blade edges. A number of tricks are employed by expert log men in grinding these double blades. One such trick is to grind one edge rounded, the other straight across. This rounded edge permits deep cuts for notching and leaves the straight edge for hewing. Another trick is to grind one edge with a chisel-type bevel one way, the other edge with the

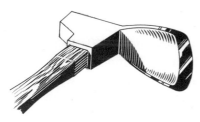

Lip-Faced Adz
(Ground with a Curve)

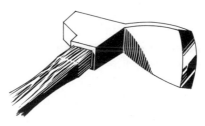

Straight-Faced Adz
(Ground Straight)

chisel-type bevel opposite. Such an instrument is also used for hewing, and the alternate grinding of the blades makes it possible to work on any side of a hewing operation without changing positions or reversing the piece being worked on. Still another trick is to put a pick on one blade while the other blade is left in its usual shape. It then looks similar to a fireman's ax. The pick end is used for handling logs. However, this pick is generally mounted on the single-bitted type of ax handle alone, and is then referred to as a picaroon. It is by far the most convenient pick, but where ax work is being done at the time of handling logs, such as limbing, the combination is desirable.

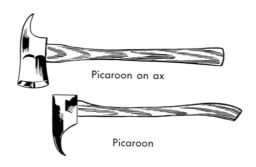

Picaroon on ax

Picaroon

These various axes are sometimes owned by log-cabin men as a full set for different applications. Some axes are single-bitted, which gives a sledge butt opposite the cutting edge, for driving wooden stakes and other uses. The handiest length in an ax for log work is what is called a "three-quarter." Some log men cut down longer-handled axes to get this "three-quarter" length, thus retaining the full-sized head with a shorter handle. A standard "three-quarter" head weighs about 2½ pounds, a full-sized ax from 3 to 6 pounds.

An **"India" oilstone** in the fine grit should be carried in the pocket to hone every cutting edge at frequent intervals. When grinding axes and other tools, one of the best methods is to use a quarter-inch electric drill and a grit-paper disk, grinding away from the edge. The final operation is honing with the "India" oilstone, and if still finer edges are wanted, finishing with a soft "Arkansas" stone.

A **broad-ax** is just what the name implies—an ax with a broad blade used for hewing to obtain flat surfaces, or for squaring timbers. The cutting edge is ground beveled, like a chisel.

A **gouge** is a chisel-like instrument with a rounded blade for accurately trimming up the rough work in the corner notching of logs.

Two types are needed—one that has the bevel of the cutting edge on the inner, or concave, side, and one that has the cutting edge on the outer, or convex, side.

**Large chisels (slicks)** are used for peeling logs.

A **caliper** is used for measuring the diameter of logs in the general selection and sorting.

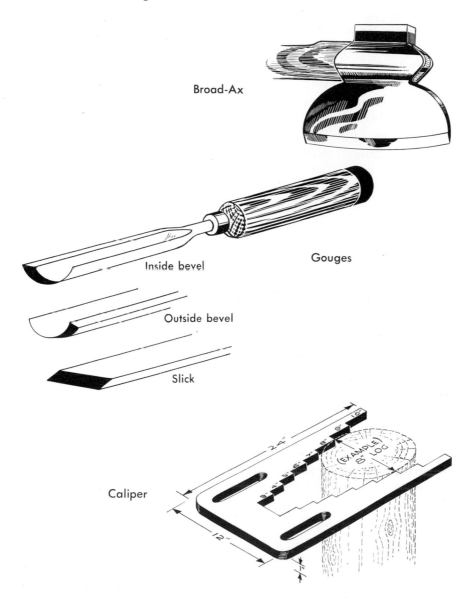

Broad-Ax

Inside bevel

Gouges

Outside bevel

Slick

Caliper

A **notching gauge, scribe, divider,** or **compass** is used for marking the notches to be made on the logs at corners and along the length of logs if contour fitting to another log is to be the method employed. Various markers are used, but the most common type is a pair of dividers made from wood provided with a coarse, heavy black crayon or pencil. This is not as accurate as the notching gauge. (See the illustration on page 115.)

**Saws** for log work are the chain saw, crosscut, "Swede" or bow saw, a coarse-toothed (about 6 to 8 teeth to the inch) carpenter's cross-cut saw, and a carpenter's ripsaw. If there is commercial electric power on the job, or a 110-volt power plant, a hand electric saw is a big time saver. A table power saw is valuable for some of the finishing-off work where lumber is used to complete the floor and roof, and where ripping is being done. However, for most small cabin work the tools are usually limited to manual types.

Pinch Bar

**Pinch bars** or **wrecking bars** are used for prying and pulling nails and spikes. Crowbars are used for heavy prying and digging.

Since the modern log cabin requires a large share of carpenter work, the tools needed for carpenter work in building the frame cabin are also needed for log-cabin work with lumber:

**Saws** for carpenter work are the crosscut, rip, miter-box, keyhole, and, in some instances, a hacksaw for cutting off nails. Here, too, electric, hand, and table saws save considerable work.

**Planes** are used for finishing off surfaces and for close fitting. A jack plane is used on the long side of lumber parallel with the grain. A block plane is used at the ends across the grain. Electric planes can be used. Rabbeting planes will cut grooves in door- and window-frame stock, but most of this is done in mills with the stock available at lumberyards.

**Hammers** are of the claw type for carpenter work. However, magnetic tack hammers for holding tacks can be used to advantage for tacking on building paper where one hand is needed for holding. A 5-pound sledge with a short handle is valuable for separating scaffold members and other such general heavy duties. A 15-pound sledge is handy for breaking up rock for concrete.

**Levels** are usually of the bubble bar type for horizontal and vertical leveling. A line level is a small aluminum unit with a bubble bulb that is hung on chalk lines for leveling footings and other long spans. A very handy and extremely accurate level that will go around objects and even level from one room to another is easily made from a piece of rubber tubing with a glass "straw" inserted at each end. The rubber tube is filled with water until it shows at both glass straws. Since water seeks a level, the water lines on the glass straws will designate two like points of desired elevation, no matter how far apart the tubes may be. In cold weather add antifreeze to the water. A transit level is extremely valuable but not essential. It is quite expensive. However, if your budget will allow you, a transit level will make the footing layout and some of the cabin work easier and more positive. A transit level is mounted on a tripod and has a sighting telescope with crosshair reticles.

**Chisels** in varying sizes from ¼ to 1½ inch are needed for setting hinges and doing other jobs.

**Nail sets** are short knurled, tapered punches for setting finishing nails below level—mostly needed in laying floors.

**Squares,** as the name implies, square the work, but also determine angles. A large 2-foot, a small 10-inch, and a bevel type are needed. The bevel type is used for marking odd angles.

A **brace** and **bits** are used for boring holes. The bits should vary from ¼ to 1 inch; and for larger holes an extension bit will be necessary. Now and then, metal drills are needed for some special purpose; and these drills can be bought with a brace shank for use with the carpenter's brace. However, this is a slow way to use a metal drill. A regular hand drill or electric drill works better. See **gimlet** (page 97).

**Wood drills** are rapid small-hole hand drills for nailing work where splitting is likely, or in hard wood where a nail would bend in driving.

**Screwdrivers** are needed for hanging doors and windows. A hand screwdriver is essential, but most of the driving of screws, once they are started, is done with a brace and a screwdriver bit.

**Carpenter pencils** have a broad flat lead that does not break as readily as that of the ordinary pencil. A knife edge can be created for accurate marking by rubbing the flat side of the lead on a piece of fine sandpaper.

**Snips** are tin shears and should be of the "duckbill" type for straight and circular cutting.

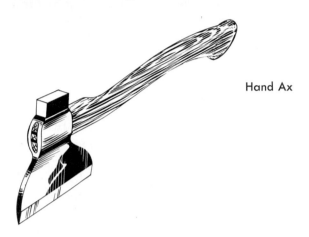

Hand Ax

**Hatchets** are used in two types—for laying wood shingles and for trimming the edges of lumber. The latter type is generally called a hand ax, having a beveled edge blade with a short handle.

**Dividers** are used for uniform spacing of various sections and for scribing round holes.

**Nail pullers** of the type used in opening wooden boxes are handy around a job where a certain amount of dismantling is generally done.

**Center punch** A special guide center punch is made for the purpose of getting screw holes in exact position when installing locks and hinges. Simple center punches mark drill holes.

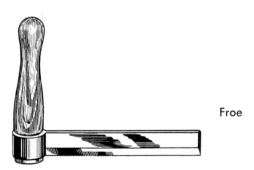

Froe

**Knives** used for trimming, such as pocket knives and sheath knives, should not be used for cutting roofing. An inexpensive knife is made for this purpose and will prevent ruining your better knives. These cheap knives have the advantage that they are soft enough to sharpen quickly with a file. A linoleum knife will also serve this purpose, and sharpens easily with a file.

**Froe**—a cleaving tool with a handle at right angles to the blade, used for splitting rough shingles or shakes from a billet of wood.

The foregoing will allow you, even with some deletions, to build a cabin without handicap.

For **stone tools** see the accompanying illustrations.

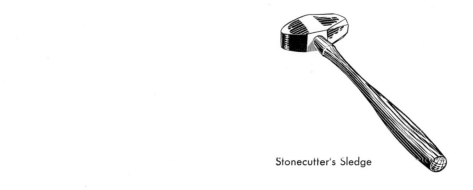

Stonecutter's Sledge

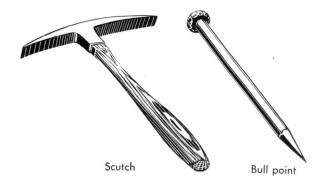

Scutch          Bull point

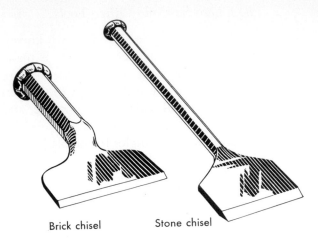

Brick chisel    Stone chisel

Pitching chisel    Serrated (toothed) chisel

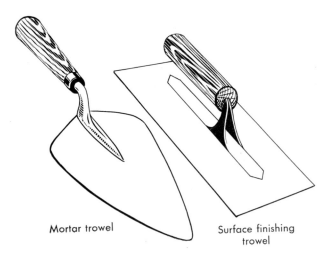

Mortar trowel    Surface finishing
trowel

# 9

## Building the Log Cabin

IF YOU CONTRACT to have your logs delivered to your building site, the chances are that they will be cut in late fall or during the winter. If possible, inspect what you buy on the stump; this will ensure your getting the best selection. Choose logs as uniform as possible from butt to top, and of even size. Logs with tops somewhere between 9 and 12 inches are best. This does not mean that logs smaller or larger in diameter cannot be used. Much will depend on the size of cabin you plan to build, and the standing timber available.

One of the most attractive and unusual cabins I have seen was made from boom logs about 16 inches in diameter. I have also seen smaller cabins made out of logs that were only 6 inches in diameter, which had their own special charm and appeal. Logs from 9 to 12 inches will be something to shoot at for size. If your logs are to run extremely long, you will probably have to settle for tops smaller than you desire.

Western cedar, pine, fir, white spruce, black spruce, tamarack (larch), and balsam make a good order of descending selection.

Logs cut in spring after the sap is up, or during the summer, peel more readily, but they check worse than logs cut in late fall or winter.

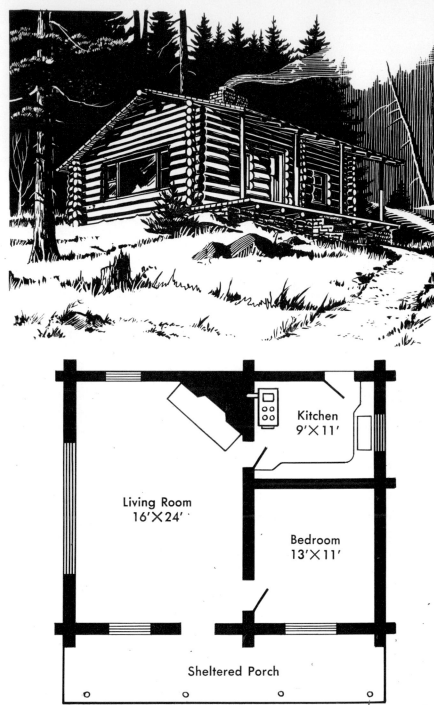

Living Room
16'×24'

Kitchen
9'×11'

Bedroom
13'×11'

Sheltered Porch

The log cabin seems most suitable to the rough mountain terrain.

Spring-cut logs are also more subject to mildew, stain discoloration, and insect attack. It is well to peel the logs as soon as they have been delivered to the site. Use a slick, an ax or adz, a spade or draw knife as a spudding tool to remove the bark. The logs should be laid well off the ground on peeled skids, with a space of 1 to 3 inches between the logs for free circulation of air. Depending on your patience and circumstance, let the logs season in this way for three months to a year; this will overcome part of the settling later when the cabin is built. The plan I like best is to cut the logs late in the fall and start building early the next fall. Then you will have good log stock. In placing the logs on skids, use only one tier if possible. If you are crowded for space, however, the logs can be piled in several tiers; but then you should place peeled poles between the tiers. Logs with slight curves should be piled so that the arc is up, and should be placed at the bottom of the pile where the weight of the other logs will help to straighten them.

If you want the logs to project beyond the cabin corners, be sure that they are from 4 to 6 feet longer than the outside of your building. If you plan to build a porch, then the sill logs, plates (top logs), purlins, and ridge logs must be long enough to extend over and beyond the porch, for porch-floor and porch-roof support.

There are many claims that certain plastic resin varnishes and compounds will keep the logs their natural light color indefinitely, but you will do well to accept this with a great deal of reservation. However, since the peeled logs will be rained on, and therefore flushed off a number of times before they are put in the wall, something is gained by coating them with a fairly strong mixture of household chlorine bleach and detergent. To some extent, this destroys the fungus that causes the blackening and staining of logs from sap.

Some enthusiastic experts maintain that the sap layer of wood should be removed with a draw knife to prevent the logs from discoloring. There are several objections to this. In the first place it is a colossal task; it destroys the smooth, natural surface of the log; and there is no real guarantee that discoloration will not occur.

Unless your logs are bought on contract, the chances are that you will be cutting them in a variety of places in order to be sure of a uniform size. The site itself scarcely ever offers what you want, and any liberal cutting of logs where your cabin is to be built will almost invariably destroy the beauty of your site.

If you are to build on a waterfront, the logs can be floated singly or rafted from considerable distances with little difficulty. This allows you a greater range of choice in the cutting, provided the logs can be purchased in this scattered manner from the government or from private sources. Cutting on government land is usually had by permit, the trees then being marked by a forestry agent.

Logs for particular uses in the cabin will vary in size. Sill logs, which receive the floor joists, should be larger in diameter than all other logs. The ridge log should be slightly smaller than the sill logs. The ridge log must be very straight. Rafters are small-diameter logs, generally called poles. They should be about half the diameter of the wall logs. Purlins (lengthwise roof supports for rafters) generally are slightly smaller than wall logs, or of the same size.

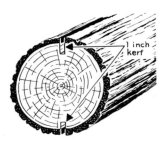

Kerf (Slot-Groove) Cut in Log with Chain Saw to Localize Checking

It can be seen that if you plan to use logs available in the area they will have to vary in diameter. Yet these variations are essential if your cabin is to have pleasing proportions. It is obvious too that logs of larger diameter have a more pleasing effect than logs of small diameter. It is also evident that large logs are harder to handle.

When the logs are delivered at the site, you may not have the time or the tools to peel them immediately. In that case, strip the bark for a width of about 2 inches along the log, from end to end, where each log joins the log above and the log below. Some of the checking will then take place along these scored areas as the logs dry—the drying period being from six months to a year. The balance of the bark can then be removed at your leisure.

In experimenting with a number of methods for the artificial control of log checking, I found one method quite promising. As the logs were stacked for the spring peeling of the bark, I used a chain saw to cut a lengthwise kerf (slot groove), about 1 inch deep and the thickness of the blade into the log, top and bottom, as the logs would be lying in the wall. This method creates an artificial release check for the

log and to a large extent allows the log to release its drying and shrinking tension at the cut groove. Because the grooves are at the joints,
they will be concealed in the wall. To keep water out of the top groove,
fill the groove with glass wool or oakum, and then seal it with calking
compound just before the log goes into the wall.

Once your logs are ready, you will proceed with the concrete footings. The illustration on page 111 shows 9 footings that have either
been set on bedrock or dug down below the frost line. If you set the

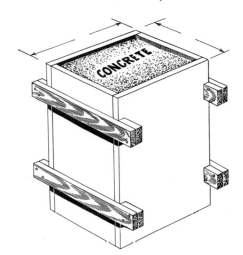

Demountable Form for
Concrete Footings

footings just below the surface, you will encounter the trouble described in Chapter 1 (page 2). The popular, picturesque setting of
log cabins on large boulders is a grave mistake, unless the boulders
disguise a concrete support footing under the boulders, extending
below the frost line. The finest log or carpentry work is sheer folly
without good footings, because of destructive frost-heaving stress.

Forms for concrete footings are simply 4 demountable sections held
together with wood cleats. (See illustration.) An average-size footing
is a column 10″ × 12″ of desired height. When footings are set into
the ground, it is well to allow a pool of concrete to form at the bottom
under the form, to give it a base larger than the footing itself. This
usually happens anyway on uneven ground, when the concrete is forced
out under the form. I usually prop up the form slightly to allow this
spreading of wet concrete at the bottom. A practice that is often overlooked, but a valuable one nevertheless, is to use a short piece of log
and tamp the earth at the bottom of the footing before setting in the
form. The chances of uniform settling are greater.

If you are to put in a full basement or a cellar, you will undoubtedly lay up the basement walls and continuous foundation with concrete blocks. This is the simplest method. A wider footing, usually about 20 inches, is poured at the base of the wall on which the concrete blocks are laid. A standard dry mortar mix, obtainable from any lumber company, is mixed with water to a stand-up thickness, applied to the footing, and the concrete block is then pressed into place. As the layers of blocks go up, they of course lap the joints on the row, or course, of blocks below. A spirit level is used constantly to keep the walls straight, and to keep the courses of blocks level. Mortar is applied with a trowel. Basement window frames are set in as the wall goes up. The basement corner blocks are laid first, and a chalk line is then stretched from corner to corner as a guide for laying the intermediate blocks. This eliminates constant leveling, although the level should be used to check everything, including the chalk-line position. (See illustration.)

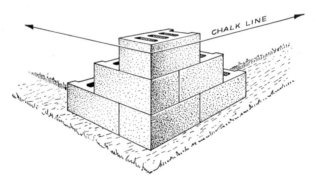

Method of Laying Concrete-Block Foundation

Full foundations, like individual footings, must also be set below the frost line. It becomes clear that continuous foundations set below the frost line are in some of the colder climates equivalent to walls of full height. It seems wasteful, when using full wall material, not to expand your excavation into a basement or cellar. Where only a cellar is to be made, the cabin can be set partly on the walls of the cellar and the rest on individual footings dug below frost level as described on page 109. On the rocky Shield of the North, and in some other regions where bedrock comes close to the surface, full foundations and footings are of course shallow.

Laying out the cabin on the ground for perfect right angles some-times causes the do-it-yourself builder trouble. The most direct way, of course, is to use a transit level; but where this is not available, the best plan is as follows: First, make certain of the general location of your proposed cabin by laying out the measurements roughly with a steel tape. Then, fully complete all of the footings to careful meas-urement along one of the long walls. These will be footings 1, 2, and 3. (See illustration.) Be sure they are all on the same level and in line. If you puddle nails into the soft concrete at the outside corners of the corner footings and at the center outer edges of the intermediate footings, and then allow them to set in the concrete, you will have ex-cellent pegs on which to hook steel tapes or to tie chalk lines for general measurements and for leveling.

Now, if you have two steel tapes handy, hook the end of one tape to the outside corner nail of footing 1, and the other tape to the out-side corner nail of footing 3. Unroll the tapes to a point beyond the opposite side wall at "A." Use the identical points of measurement on both tapes. A line drawn from the center of footing 2 to the point held by your two tapes is the center line of your cabin.

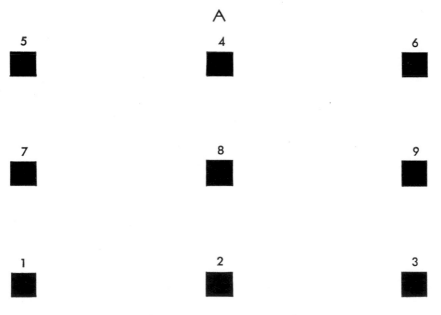

Method of Laying Out Footings

If you measure along this center line from the middle of the outside edge of footing 2, the width of your cabin foundation, you can put in footing 4 on this center line. After putting in footing 4, you can put in footing 5 simply by measuring the width of your cabin from 1 to 5, and half the length of your cabin from 4 to 5. You can put in footing 6 by measuring the width of your cabin from 3 to 6, and half the length of your cabin from 4 to 6.

All final intermediate footings, such as 7, 8, and 9, can be put in simply by stretching a chalk line from the corner footings.

If you do not have two steel tapes, use your one tape and a piece of stovepipe wire on which you have marked the measurement with a pearl of solder or a dot of white paint. Never use a cord for this type of measurement. It stretches.

Chalk lines can be set up for all footings before any footings are put in, but you will then have to hurdle these lines. However, if you wish to put up chalk lines all around, you can use the same general principle to get a perfect rectangle, using stakes to fasten the chalk lines. These stakes are placed beyond the corners, the chalk lines then crossing at the exact corners of the cabin footings or foundation. Tie the chalk lines together where they cross at each corner.

You can use any of various methods for obtaining a perfect rectangle or square in laying out the foundation or footings if you make the following check of dimensions. A cabin will be a perfect rectangle or square if, after finding that the dimensions of the foundation are correct, you also find that the diagonals from corner to corner are exactly the same.

After the footings are in and have set up hard, you will lay your sill logs. It is well to let the footings set for a few days before laying the sills. This avoids any breaking off of soft concrete footing corners by rough contact. In fact, it is best if the footings can be put in and left for a considerable time. I have, on occasion, poured the footings in the fall and started the cabin proper in the spring.

With the footings in, you are now ready to start your log work. Remember that in log-cabin construction your dimensions are made on the inside walls of the cabin. On frame cabins the dimensions are taken on the outside. As you will readily see, the inside face of the logs should all line up in a vertical plane, while the outside wall can vary from log to log.

Flatten the underside of your sill logs so that they will lie steady on the footings. Lay the sill logs level, with the inside edges parallel, and to inside building dimensions. Roll the two end logs into their proper places. Be sure that these logs lie with the inside edges parallel and true to inside building dimensions. Scribe all four corners on both sides of the end logs, in the manner shown in the illustration. Roll these end logs over and cut out the major part of the wood for the notch with a sharp ax, leaving the scribed lines still showing. (It is a good idea to go over these lines again with a crayon or indelible pencil, so that the lines will be distinct.) Now, take your outside-beveled gouge and clean out the notch up to the scribed lines. The notch should wind up somewhat cupped, so that the edges of your notching will fit flush against the lower log—in this first instance, against the sill logs.

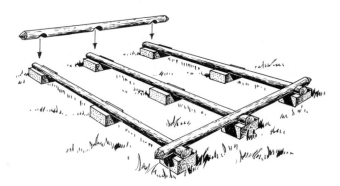

Laying the Sills and First End Logs

So far, you have no parallel fitting of one log against the other. The sills rest on the concrete footings, the end logs across the sill logs. (See illustration.)

At this point, without a wall to interfere, you had better make provision for your floor joists; otherwise you will be in an awkward position to work. Two general methods are used for setting in the floor. If you plan to make your floor joists out of round poles instead of planks, you will have to notch the sills and square the ends of your pole floor joists to fit these notches. If you use planks and the method in the first illustration on page 114, you will save yourself a lot of work that will, in any event, be buried beneath the permanent floor. If you use the method in the second illustration on page 114 I suggest you obtain a chain saw to do the notching; otherwise you are in for a tedious job of cutting out these notches. After the notches are sawed out, the wood is removed with a chisel.

The top side of the round floor joists must be flattened to receive the subfloor. This can be done with an ax or adz. The simplest method is to put the pole floor joists in pairs on sawhorses and run a chain-saw blade between them. This flattens two at a time. If an even flatter surface is needed, repeat the chain-saw operation.

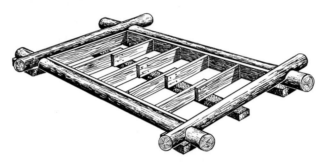

Method of Setting In Floor Joists of Planks

If you have a continuous foundation, and not individual footings, the entire floor-joist assembly can rest on the foundation. But since you will have to cut away a portion of your sill logs to reach the top inner edge of this foundation, it is not very practical because of the

Method of Setting In Floor Joists of Round Logs

amount of labor involved. The method in the first illustration on page 114 is a lot simpler and easier in construction, and is practical. The floor-joist assembly as shown is set in after the floor joists are nailed to the planks. Once the two assemblies are in, they can then be nailed to the sills.

I might say at this point that a great deal of theory in log-cabin building involves elaborate notching-in of floor joists, cutting voids for splines, mortising, and complex fitting of parts. Generally, this never gets beyond the theoretical stage of illustrations in a magazine article or a book. Admittedly, where there is no limit to time or expense, this kind of work is interesting—in fact fascinating. But for practical log-cabin building, it is neither essential nor does it necessarily increase the structural value.

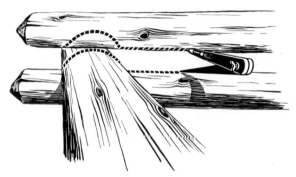

Scribing the Logs for Notching and Parallel Fit

In the early days, in even the most ordinary type of dwelling all floor joists were mortised into a sill—a job usually done indoors in winter. That was in a day when labor costs were negligible. In our day it would be an extravagance with little or no gain. This is not a matter of good workmanship but of economy in structural principles. This is important where your time and budget are factors.

Now that you have the two end logs in place over the sill logs and the floor taken care of, you can proceed with your side-wall logs. These logs are rolled into their exact parallel positions, determined by the inside measurements of your cabin. Scribe them in the same manner as you did your end logs; but here you have an additional scribing job. Each of these side-wall logs must fit for its entire length against the log below it. Use your divider, resting it on the log below, and scribe the entire length of the log above, according to the contours of the log below. Besides notching out the corners as you did with your end logs, you must take your adz, or ax, and cut away enough of the underside of the scribed log above, so that it will fit the contours of the log below. This should be a channel, cut with an ax or lip-faced adz, from end to end of the log, so that the edges of the channel-like groove come together against the log below.

This is the hand-wrought, structural method of fitting logs along their parallel sides and it is so laborious, compared to fitting them by means of a chain saw, that today it seems almost unbearably tedious. I am fully aware that sentimentally there is much in favor of this construction of a log cabin entirely by the old-fashioned manual method, and this point of view I respect highly. On the other hand, it seems to me that where your time is precious, you should conserve it; and where there are short cuts to the same end, you should take them, unless your project is a leisure-time hobby. My own feeling is that in any log-cabin project the combination of the old manual method with the modern machine type of construction is permissible if it can give you the best results.

The chain-saw method of fitting logs parallel is as follows: Before the logs are placed in the wall, wherever two logs are to be fitted full length along their parallel tops and bottoms, they should be laid side by side on sawhorses, with the logs held together with log dogs in the required position; the blade of a chain saw is then run between them. This cuts away all humps and bows that prevent closing the gap between the logs. The first cut may not do the job. In that case, the log dogs should be removed, the logs brought together, and redogged, and the chain-saw blade again run between them. Ill-fitting logs may require several such cuttings.

When using this operation, you must plan several logs ahead. No logs should go into the wall that have not first been treated with the chain saw, top and bottom, for parallel fit. A strip of glass wool placed between the logs as the wall goes up will create a tight, invisible seal.

Once the logs are given this parallel fit, they are rolled into position and notched by hand, in the same general manner as already described. Logs can, of course, be fitted at the corner with the chain saw as shown in the illustration, but this type of corner has not had much appeal for the log-cabin builder who favors the time-approved saddle corner.

Method of Notching Corners with the Chain Saw

Never fit the logs with the chain saw after they are placed in the wall. The fitting will interfere with the notching operation. Moreover, a chain saw used in various awkward positions at heights on scaffolds is not advisable for safety reasons, and tends to increase the amount of over-all labor. Fitting the logs together, parallel, while they are on skids or sawhorses, speeds up the operation, gives a better job, and makes the notching operation more positive.

If you do not care to buy a chain saw, you can rent one. Since this will be on a time basis, the work for parallel fitting and most other uses of the chain saw can be done on a precutting basis, the logs and pieces numbered with crayon, and the saw returned. Logs for parallel walls should be numbered 1, 3, 5, 7, and so on. Logs at right angles to these should be numbered 2, 4, 6, 8, and so on.

The inside wall should be kept plumb by a level and a board used to maintain the vertical wall. Disregard the exterior. As the wall goes up, the successive tiers of logs should be kept sufficiently level so that when you reach the top of the wall there will not be more than an inch of variation along the top level of your logs when you begin to frame up the roof. Measure up from the floor joists as you go.

Keep the height of the corners the same, as each tier of logs is laid.

Regulating the height of the corners is effected by reversing the top and butt ends of the logs in the various tiers.

Where the cabin is large, the logs should be spiked together or doweled with wooden pins. This spiking or doweling should be done through each log, 2 to 3 feet from the notched corners, and the same distance from doors and windows. Obviously, the spiking or doweling should be slightly staggered, otherwise one spike will be driven into another below it.

Succeeding Courses of Logs as the Wall Goes Up

Spiking or doweling does not interfere with settling. Where dowels are used, they slip enough to allow the logs to settle. In spiking, a hole of a size that will readily admit the head of the spike is first bored halfway through the upper part of the log. Then a smaller hole of a size that will allow a snug fit for the shank of the spike is bored the rest of the way through the log. As the wall settles, the logs slip along the

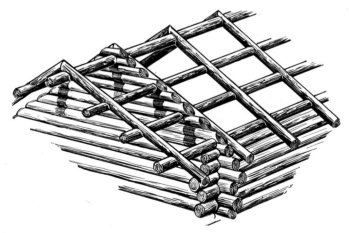

General Roof Assembly Showing Purlins, Rafters, Ridge and Gable Construction

spike, allowing the logs to close up. The size of the log will determine the length of the spikes, but spikes up to 12 inches can be bought. Sections of steel rod cut to length can be used instead of spikes. The spike or rod is driven into the logs with a 5-pound hammer, and when the head reaches the top of the log it is driven as far as required with a punch held against the head of the spike.

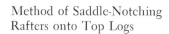
Method of Saddle-Notching
Rafters onto Top Logs

When you reach the gables, the process of log assembly changes substantially. Here, log upon log is piled and spiked into place without the corner notching, until you reach the ridge. These gable logs rapidly get shorter as you go up the gable, until you reach a height where a purlin needs to go in. (See illustration on page 118.) The next gable log is then fitted at both ends around the purlin with an ax or adz and an inside-beveled gouge.

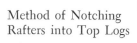
Method of Notching
Rafters into Top Logs

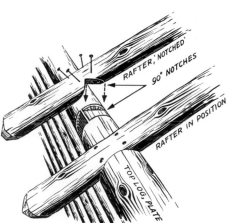

Usually, there are two or three purlins used on each side of the roof, if the roof is to have rafters and is to be sheathed with boards. If shingles or shakes are used directly on the purlins, a purlin goes in at every other gable log. Or purlin logs can be laid side by side across the entire roof, without rafters, to receive the shakes or shingles. These are simply variations and can be left to your personal choice of construction.

Where purlins cover the entire roof, they need not be notched into the gable logs or given a parallel fit, but merely piled side by side on the roof slope against the edges of the gable and spiked into place. Shingles or shakes are then laid on these logs. Any openings between them have no effect on the tightness of the roof, once the shingles or shakes are laid. However, if you wish, you can run the chain-saw blade between the purlins just as you did with the wall logs.

No notching is required for the gable logs, but parallel fitting by chain-saw or by hand in the same way as with the wall logs is necessary.

When you reach the ridge of your cabin, you will of course set in the ridge log. It must coincide with the slope of your rafters.

If you have decided to use the widely spaced purlin method of construction, you will now proceed to put up your rafters. These rafters are notched to fit into the top logs in your side walls. Two practical methods are commonly used. (See illustrations on page 119.)

The top ends of your rafters are notched with a gouge, having the bevel on the inner edge so as to fit neatly against and around the ridge logs. Here the rafters are spiked into place. You will also spike the rafters where they are notched into the top plate or top wall logs. Sometimes the rafters are notched for fitting to the purlins. This added labor is not really necessary if the purlins are set low enough so that the rafters just rest on them. (See illustration on page 118.)

Here again we come back to the chain saw. If you run the chain-saw blade between pairs of rafters as they lie on skids or sawhorses, a nailing surface for the roof boards can be provided. If the same treatment with a chain saw is given the opposite side of the rafters where they rest against the purlins, they generally provide an even contact with the purlins, with very little trimming necessary. There is some objection to this, however, since the area surfaced by the chain saw will show on the inside of the cabin.

The ridge log, plate logs, and purlins will extend far enough beyond

Shingle Flashing for Roof Hip

the gable walls to support the overhang of the roof and the so-called "floating" rafters that form a part of this overhang. If a porch platform with a generous roof overhang is to be a part of the structure, these ridge and plate logs, along with the purlins and top plate logs, will have to be extended to form a large part of the porch roof sup-

Shingle Flashing for Roof Valley

port. Brackets or porch poles, of course, may be added for such support, and lend an attractive appearance. Sills will be extended too, to support porch floor joists.

After you have nailed down the rafters, your next step will be to nail on your roof boards, and then lay your roofing or shingles on these boards. (See illustrations on page 121.)

If you have decided to saw out your windows and doors after laying up the logs, then you will mark the window and door openings on the completed walls with a level and crayon. You should then nail a board guide along the crayon marks, and saw out the openings. A chain saw greatly facilitates this operation. On the other hand, you may have decided to make your door and window openings as you progressed with your log work, setting in shorter pieces of logs at either side of your door and window openings as you went along. The loose log ends are then braced with vertical board supports, and nailed alongside the loose log ends until you are ready to frame in the openings. Finally, the log ends, left uneven at the openings, are sawed down the line of the board supports for straight framing areas.

Your fireplace opening should either be allowed for in the wall where this piece of masonry is to go, or sawed out later as the construction goes up. If the opening is allowed for during construction, board supports for the log ends will be required just as in your supporting window and door openings. For information regarding the cutting of a chimney opening for a stove, see Chapter 10, "Building the Frame Cabin."

If you want your log cabin to have an authentic look, then you should make your door and window frames on the job from planks. The inside facing of these plank frames will have half-inch lumber nailed to them for door and window stops, properly called the rim or jamb against which the door or window closes. The plank that fits at the bottom of a door or window frame to form the sill will be wider than the rest of the frame and will slope slightly downward to allow rain to run off. Though planks with rabbeted stops can be bought at lumberyards for custom-made doors and windows, thus somewhat simplifying the construction, they have too formal a look to be completely acceptable. If you insist on having windows and doors factory-made, suggest a simple cabin type of frame to the manufacturer.

Provision must be made in the frames for inside and outside windows if storm windows are to be used, and in warm seasons for screens and windows. This is already taken care of in the rabbeted plank stock available at lumberyards.

Screens are a problem when you want your windows to swing outward. Windows that swing outward are better in principle for shedding blowing rain, and are out of the way when open, but this arrangement puts the screens on the inside. If screens are on the inside, special hardware for opening the windows through the screen frame will have to be bought. If you use simple catches, the screens can be hung on hinges—but it will be necessary to open and close the screens every time you open and close the outside windows.

Inside windows are quite commonly hinged at the top and are swung upward and out of the way, thus allowing the use of outside screens. Where the windows can be swung back against an inside wall, this arrangement is more convenient. Drip caps are needed along the lower part of the sash on inside-type windows to prevent leaks.

Doors for log cabins are most effectively made from planks or boards with wood battens and rustic hardware. Wood door latches are in keeping with plank or board doors, because they are primitive and always interesting.

There now are prefabricated log cabins that can be constructed in a day. Every part, from basic logs to roof and chimney, comes fabricated and "packaged," ready to be assembled. The ax, adz, and gouge lie unromantically dormant in the tool chest—forgotten where this type of cabin is concerned. However, the excellent saddle-notch principle, previously described, has been retained at the corners of these machine-age cabins. It has, apparently, withstood the test of time as the best possible notching method.

I referred earlier to the elaborate theories of using splines and other complex fitting for door and window frames, on rafters and in other places—theories that are rarely put in practice or even understood. Where the prefabricated log cabin is concerned, fast-cutting rabbeting and milling machines cut every conceivable rabbet, groove, notch, inlet, and spline so that when the pieces are delivered to the job all fit together perfectly, like a wooden toy puzzle.

Here the do-it-yourself builder has a heyday. He can erect his cabin without outside help in a few days at the most. He will still have to put in concrete footings or a foundation of cement blocks set below the frost line. But from then on, the job is only that of piling one log on top of another, with no thought of fit, notching, or channeling.

Each log will fit as though it had been poured into place. The reason is obvious: Logs, seasoned scientifically and kiln dried, are run through milling machines until the parallel joining is so precise that the log below fits into a perfectly milled round channel in the log above. There are novel variations in this parallel fitting. All sorts of patented rabbeted joints are provided to close the space between the logs, depending on the caprice of the manufacturer.

The only objection to cabins of machine-made logs is that they are too perfect. The artful effect of a log cabin built by your own hands is that it does not appear machine-perfect. Machine refinements only emphasize that your cabin has not been made by fine handwork. One way of overcoming this is to trim off the neatly cut log ends with an ax to make them uneven. At least the resulting design is reminiscent of old-time hand construction.

Prefabricated log cabins are now made in many parts of the country. You should inquire therefore at your local lumberyard for the nearest mill that makes them, and thus save freight costs.

To seal joints between logs when using the chain-saw method, place a strip of glass-wool insulation between the logs as they are laid. This will be regarded as "chinking," though it's a far cry from the old method of tamping various materials into the wide openings between logs. Glass wool is an everlasting material that seals out insects and weather. Where corner notching will allow it, by virtue of a not too close fit of the logs, or in the cupping of corner notches, it is well to insert glass wool at these points too, and in any other void that needs sealing off.

For chinking by the old method where logs are given a parallel fit with hand tools, a tarred sisal or hemp, called "oakum," is used. Most of the chinking is then done after the logs are in the walls, when the oakum is pounded in with a thin billet of wood and a hammer. If it is possible to lay some of the oakum chinking as the logs go up, this saves time and labor later. Calking compound is sometimes used to seal the joints completely after chinking with oakum. While calking compound is not necessary when the chain saw and glass wool are used, where a neat, hermetically sealed joint is desired, the compound can be applied with a calking gun and a narrow, pointed trowel.

Various oils and stains are used on logs. Some of the new plastic glazes have proved successful in keeping logs their new, natural color.

The clear types of varnishes can be darkened with burnt umber or raw sienna. The interior can be treated with a coat of clear shellac to prevent wood resins and pitch from oozing out, and then given a coat or two of flat varnish.

Badly discolored logs can be refinished with log-cabin paint. This is a heavy cream-colored paint that, when dry, is given a stain glaze-coat that goes on unevenly, giving the effect of wood grain. At a distance it resembles new wood—if not inspected too closely.

Earlier (page 10), reference was made to hand-split shakes as a picturesque roof covering. These are not difficult to make. Cedar is the best material if clear western cedar logs are obtainable that do not contain knots. Clear pine will do, but it rots quicker than cedar, and should be dipped in clear creosote as a preservative. The logs are cut into 24″ chunks. They can be cut shorter than this, but less than 18″ would be impractical for proper lap.

A tool called a "froe" is used for splitting billets or chunks of wood into shakes. See the illustration of the froe on page 102. The froe blade is set on the end of the wood chunk, and the blade is struck with a wooden mallet. The shake thickness should be kept to about a half-inch or a little thicker. The chunk will have to be turned end-to-end where the grain tends to run off at an angle. The best shakes are thinner at one end than at the other, but this is not absolutely essential.

# 10

## Building the Frame Cabin

THE TERM "FRAME" is used to identify cabins built of lumber as against cabins built of logs, stone, brick, and other materials. "Plywood" cabins are included in this chapter, since such cabins basically come under the heading of "frame" cabins.

The instructions for foundations shown in Chapter 9, "Building the Log Cabin," apply equally to the foundations for frame cabins, and will not be repeated here.

When putting in sills and floor joists, the first thing to keep in mind is that the floor size of the cabin must be in an even number of feet —no length or width of the building should be an odd number of feet. The reason for this is that most lumber comes in even-numbered lengths. There is an exception. Studs are sold in 7-foot lengths. This permits the cabin height to be an uneven number of feet, but since only the width of the studs is involved here, there is no problem. If the cabin must have an odd number in any of its linear dimensions, be sure that your lumber can be cut without waste. For example, if you need 7- and 9-foot lengths, buy 16-foot lumber to be sawed into these lengths.

The sills for your cabin, which are 2-inch planks of the same width and thickness as your floor joists, are the members to which you will nail your floor joists. I have found it good practice to double and lap the sills to overcome the problem of splicing over each footing. Construction becomes easier and stronger. Sills can be single if the footings are properly spaced to hold the spliced joint. Where sills are single, the sill planks are abutted, and a piece of plank or board is nailed across the joint on the inside of the sills between two joists.

The first operation in building your cabin of lumber is to make a frame from your sills the size of your footings, setting the sills on edge over the outer rim of these footings.

Here you are apt to make your first mistake. As I have already mentioned, dimensions should be kept in an even number of feet. If you were now to nail your sills together as they came in these even numbers from the lumberyard, you would have odd dimensions for the reason that the thickness of the planks will have been added to the even dimensions. To overcome this mistake, determine what the actual outside even dimensions of the cabin will be when it is finished, complete with wall boards, insulating felt, and siding. This final dimension then will be your even number. Incidentally, you will saw off enough from the sill planks and floor joists to allow for the combined thickness of planks, wall boards, insulating felt, and siding to get your total dimensions in an even number.

If you find that the final dimensions of your finished cabin add up to even numbers on the outside, you are on the right track. If you did not take this cutting of the sills and floor joists into consideration, you can see that because wall boards and siding also come in 2-foot multiples in length, they would be too short to reach across your walls, and if they were spliced they would come out uneven, causing considerable waste of lumber.

When your floor joists have been nailed into place and properly squared up, bolt down the sill and floor joist assembly to triangular pieces of plank nailed into the inside corners of the sills over the footings. Bore a hole into the pieces of plank through which the bolt will pass. Another method which is even better in principle, and stronger, is to drive spikes through the sills at the corners, then pour concrete into the corners to cover the protruding spikes and the bolt. Common baling wire can be twisted around the spikes and bolt to reinforce the concrete.

Your next operation is to lay the rough floor or subfloor, using shiplap, boards, or plywood. If you are to use the cabin only for summer, you will not need a subfloor. In that case lay the finished flooring at right angles to and directly on the floor joists. If you are to double the floor, the rough floor must be laid diagonally. This will permit you to lay the finished floor lengthwise or crosswise, as the shape of the cabin warrants. By so doing the top floor always crosses the joints in the subfloor. If plywood is used for the subfloor, no problem exists. The sheets can be laid in any direction to suit the plywood sheets and floor-joist spacings, which generally are 16 inches from center to center of the joists.

The walls are now ready to go up. If the cabin is not too large, you will nail your wall studs to your bottom and top plates as they lie on the floor, and then raise the whole assembly at once, sliding the assembly over to the edge of your floor, raising it, and nailing it down through the bottom plate. The studs will be 16 inches apart in the wall, except at window and door openings, where the spacing will be made to receive these frames.

Cross members, "headers," will go above and below your window-frames. These can go in before or after you raise the wall assembly. They must be set in, properly squared. My experience has been that it is easier to do this while the stud assembly is still on the floor.

Window and door frames for a rugged frame cabin should be of the same general pattern as that recommended for log cabins.

The stud assemblies for all four walls are, as described, made on the floor, raised into place, each individually and temporarily braced to hold them in position, and then finally nailed together at the corners. A top plate is then added, lapping over onto the adjoining walls. Before nailing, be sure that the wall assemblies are plumb in both directions. (See illustration.)

If the cabin is to be paneled on the inside, an extra stud will be needed to create a nailing corner. This calls for a slight trick in arrangement, shown in the illustration.

Now that your four wall-stud assemblies are up, you will need to put on part, or all, of the sheathing in order to brace the walls securely while you erect the roof rafters. Wall sheathing can be plywood, shiplap, common boards, or pressed board. If you are in a hurry to get a roof overhead for protection against rough weather, you can put on only enough sheathing to brace the wall securely, leaving the remainder of the sheathing to be finished later.

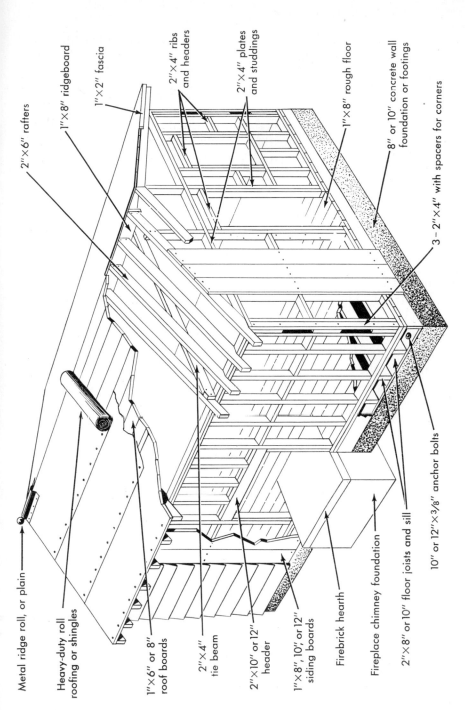

2"×6" rafters

1"×8" ridgeboard

1"×2" fascia

2"×4" ribs and headers

2"×4" plates and studdings

1"×8" rough floor

8" or 10" concrete wall foundation or footings

3 – 2"×4" with spacers for corners

10" or 12"×3/8" anchor bolts

2"×8" or 10" floor joists and sill

Fireplace chimney foundation

Firebrick hearth

1"×8", 10", or 12" siding boards

2"×10" or 12" header

2"×4" tie beam

1"×6" or 8" roof boards

Heavy-duty roll roofing or shingles

Metal ridge roll, or plain

Complete Frame Cabin Structural Assembly Diagram

If you have established the pitch angle of your roof on paper, or from your miniature cabin model, you are now ready to notch your rafters where they fit on the top plate—on top of the wall and where they join the ridge. Obviously the angles of the notching must fit the angle of the roof pitch. If you are adept at figures and the use of the carpenter's square, you will be able to calculate these angles mathematically. If not, it doesn't matter. Simply use two ordinary boards of the same width as your rafter planks. Have someone hold the boards up in place while you go off at a distance to study the angle. Change the angle several times until it pleases you. Then, while the boards are held in this position, take a level and mark the angles on the boards, both at the ridge center and at the top of the wall. If there is no one to hold the boards for you, use a steel clamp at the ridge and support the boards with braces, changing the angle until you like it. The lower end of your rafters at the extreme eaves will be sawed off on a straight line after all rafters are in, using a stretched chalk line to mark them.

Be sure that your ridgeboard is at dead center. Carefully notch out one of the boards with a saw and use it for a pattern, marking and notching all the roof rafters alike. A good idea is to set up the first pair of rafters after you have notched them, to be sure you have made no mistake. Always try out everything in a practical way, if possible. Theory sometimes becomes complicated, especially where angles are concerned.

Because rafters are set on edge at the plates, the only way to fasten them is by toe-nailing. You can buy, at any lumberyard, the inexpensive metal cleats that fasten the rafters to the top plate by a secure nailing principle.

If you use a ridgeboard or plank to which you nail the upper end of your rafters—and you should—you must allow for the thickness of this board when you cut the length of the rafters. (Sometimes rafter is nailed to rafter—a poor method in my estimation, because it generally causes misalignment of the ridge.) A ridgeboard or plank is also a guide for your rafters, allows a straighter ridge, and makes the nailing job of the rafters at the ridge easier, better in principle, and more substantial. If you use heavy timber rafters, and plan to have these timber rafters showing for effect on the underroof ceiling, the ridgeboard should be a 2- or 3-inch-thick plank to give it a rugged appearance in keeping with the timber rafters.

The ridgeboard gives better nailing support, and lends a more effective interior.

The only difference in the addition of a ridgeboard or plank is that you cut each rafter a bit shorter, an amount equal to half the thickness of your ridgeboard. (See illustration.)

Once the rafters are up, you will lay the roof sheathing, which can be shiplap, boards, or plywood, and soon thereafter lay the shingles or roofing. Before laying the shingles or roofing, you must of course make provision for a chimney. It is best to do this while you are in the process of laying the sheathing. Simply cut a square hole through the roof sheathing, and frame it up between the studs with the same 2-inch plank material, as the studs themselves. (See illustration showing method for flashing around a chimney, suitable for both shingles and roofing, on page 72.)

If you do not plan to have a regular ceiling, and intend finishing off the underside of your rafters with inside paneling, you can of course lay your insulation between the roof rafters. If you would rather use timbers for rafters and have these show on the inside, you can nail inside paneling on the upper side of the timbers, where it will be visible inside the cabin between the rafters. Then nail 2 $\times$ 4's flat on the top side of the paneling over every rafter, and after insulating between the 2 $\times$ 4's sheath over your roof and lay your roofing.

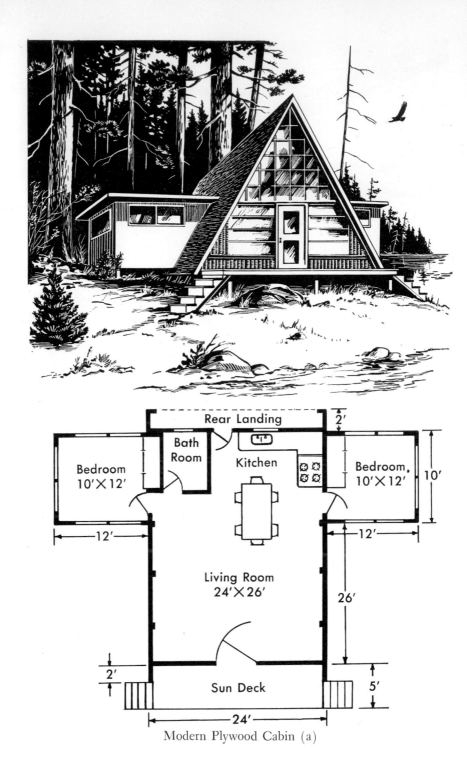

Modern Plywood Cabin (a)

If you plan a regular flat ceiling, it is a good idea to put in your ceiling joists as soon as you have your rafters up, otherwise you will have trouble getting them in their full length. They should be 2 × 6's, but 2 × 4's can be used if they are braced to the ridge. They are set on edge on the top plate and nailed to the rafters.

A timbered, paneled ceiling is most attractive. Here you can economize by putting in timbers as joists or supports for the ceiling, and then nailing the ceiling paneling on top of the timbers. The timbers should be spaced well. The problem arises as to how to get the last few pieces of paneling on the timbers and the insulation put in without nailing yourself into the attic. If you leave part of the sheathing off one gable, you have an escape route. And if you want to use the attic for storage, you can put in a trap door that pushes up from below to allow yourself an exit.

You can now set in your window and door frames, hang your doors and windows, clean out the sawdust and waste lumber from the interior, and move in. Wall siding and interior finish can be put on at your leisure. Remember, the application of siding, shingles, and roofing starts at the bottom. With shingles you double the first course. Each course covers the nail heads of the previous course.

If possible, roofing should be laid, weighted with planks, and allowed to expand and flatten in the heat for a day or two, then nailed down. Naturally, this applies only to roll roofing and not to shingles. Roll roofing laps the ridge and needs no ridge cap. Shingles require a metal ridge, or one made from a pole channeled with a lip adz.

The various assemblies from footings to roof, taken in their proper order, illustrate that the building process is not complicated and is well within the scope of anyone who has a little manual skill. Furthermore, the tools needed to build the average frame cabin are comparatively few. See Chapter 8, "The Chain Saw and Other Tools."

Plywood cabins, though classed as frame cabins, are really developing into a new and novel type of their own. The values of this type of construction are its tensile strength, its extreme lightness, and its speedy construction. It can almost be said that with a few dimensional support pieces and a few sheets of plywood, you have material for a cabin. This is, of course, not quite true; but walls, roof, floor, and partitions are now being made with supports and plywood, independent of many other current building materials.

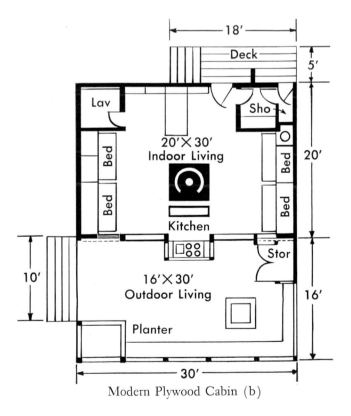

Modern Plywood Cabin (b)

One of the first questions you may ask yourself about this type of cabin is, "Won't it be carried off by the first strong wind?" The answer is "No." If the structure is bolted to concrete footings, the plywood has exceptional strength to resist the elements. An important thing to remember is that plywood adds greatly to the strength of the supporting dimensional pieces to which the plywood is nailed. We have a good example of this well adapted principle of construction in the accompanying illustration.

There are two types of plywood, outside and inside, the outside plywood being bonded with waterproof glue. The difference in cost is considerable, but even where plywood is used indoors, if it is to be subjected to high humidity the waterproof outside plywood should always be used, to prevent the laminations pulling apart.

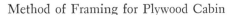

Method of Framing for Plywood Cabin

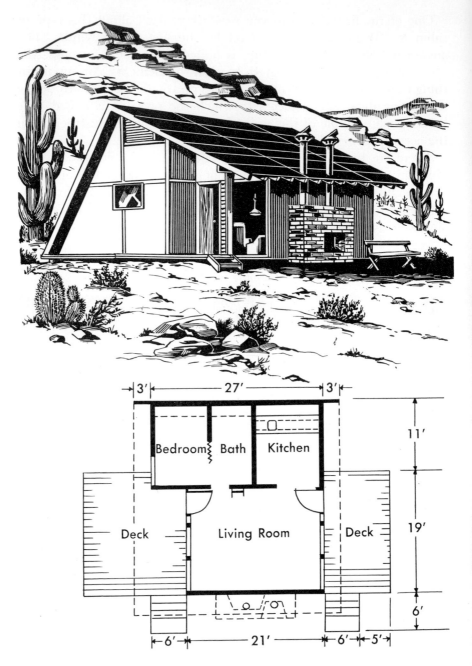

The plywood cabin adapts itself well to the southwest.

When figuring the cost of plywood, the low cost of applying it should also be considered. The sheets being large, it goes without saying that much labor is saved in sheathing over large areas.

Plywood construction should be given serious consideration for cabins in those warm regions of the Southwest where little heating is required. This might seem to be in contradiction to the need for insulation against heat. If residence is maintained throughout the year, the need for insulation and air-conditioning equipment is obvious, but for those who seek desert living where nights are cool and days are lived in the open, plywood is the solution to low-budget building and living.

This does not mean that plywood will not adapt itself to life in the North. Here, as in air-conditioned houses in the South, walls can be of plywood, doubled and insulated.

The use of large plywood sheets for exteriors at one time created a monotonous effect. This has been largely overcome by creating interesting panel sections with recessed trim, thus breaking up the flat surfaces of exterior walls. Attractive siding effects are cut into the surface of plywood sheets. These are generally kerfs, rabbets, or molding designs. Now large panels used in combination with siding-faced plywood, placed both vertically or horizontally in architectural design, have opened up almost a new era in plywood cabin exteriors.

Interiors in any type of cabin lend themselves well to the use of plywood. Here large plain or surface-cut panels are distinctively made of fine woods, such as walnut, maple, cedar, and mahogany.

Cabins of plain plywood sheets can be finished off on the outside with any type of siding desired, with the plywood used only as sheathing and structural support. Insulation for deadening sound between rooms is a major consideration in plywood cabins, but deadening felt and insulation readily solve this problem.

However, where families are large, where two or more generations are to occupy the same cabin, or where visitors will be a factor, it is usually a better plan to reduce the cabin size and construct two or more separate cabins. The so-called "guest cabin" has been a great success.

A plan that has been given much consideration in modern cabin design is that of developing a central cabin unit of such proportions

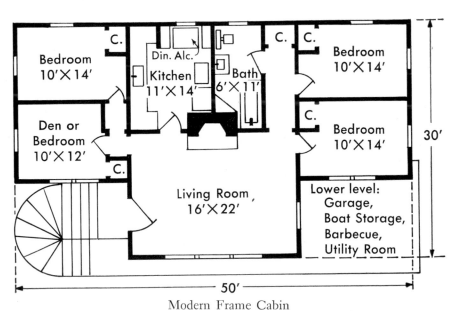

Bedroom
10'×14'

C.

Din. Alc.

Kitchen
11'×14'

Bath
6'×11'

C.

C.

Bedroom
10'×14'

Den or
Bedroom
10'×12'

C.

C.

Bedroom
10'×14'

Living Room
16'×22'

Lower level:
Garage,
Boat Storage,
Barbecue,
Utility Room

30'

50'

Modern Frame Cabin

and dimensions as will permit later addition of one or more wings. This "rambler" principle is generally very effective architecturally. Wings have the advantage of separating the living quarters of the occupants, and of giving privacy.

Outside doors to bedrooms enable early risers to depart without disturbing the household. Where separate cabins are the choice, small kitchenette areas enable your guests and you to enjoy those periods of privacy so important in prolonged human relationships.

# 11

## Fireplaces and Other Heating Units

THE OPEN FIRE, for its warmth and social cheer, is as important today in the domestic circle as it was in primitive man's time. An open fireplace of some kind should be an integral part of your cabin plans.

Had this chapter been written twenty or thirty years ago, you would have had to educate yourself in a number of formidable problems such as smoke, smoke shelves, the explosion of stone from excessive heat, to name only a few that would have kept you tossing in your sleep before you plucked up enough courage to begin the building of your first fireplace. Today you have been freed from many of these early bugbears by commercial accessories that make your job easier and the practical result more certain of success. But in any event, your fireplace footing or foundation will have to be of poured concrete or laid cement blocks set below the frost line, otherwise, eventually you will have trouble.

Well meaning friends may tell you, "Go ahead, set it on the ground and save yourself a lot of work." If you do, and the frost cracks the whole fireplace from stack to hearth, creating a serious fire hazard, you might as well move and get rid of both fireplace and friends, because there isn't much you can do to salvage either. No more foolish

Concrete Fireplace Footing Showing Method of Supporting Floor Joists

advice can be given you, and there is no surer way to court disaster.

Begin by digging down below the frost line. Build a wooden form for pouring a concrete crib the size of your fireplace base, or build up this crib with cement blocks as already described in the setting of cabin footings and foundations (page 110). Fill the completed concrete crib with sand and gravel—not dirt. Tamp the sand or gravel down solid, using a timber. Then pour a concrete slab over the top. You will need some reinforcing iron in the slab, but don't get too technical. I put an old-fashioned bedspring in my first slab for reinforcement. After thirty years it is still as sound as a hound's tooth. Hog-fence wire is good, or any iron rods picked up in the nearest junkyard. If you have the work done for you by a mason, he will probably not have time to hunt up these money savers and will put in standard reinforcing rods. (See illustration.)

With the slab finished, you now have something solid on which to set your fireplace. A layer of firebrick is needed over the slab to withstand heat and protect the slab. At this point, you can either build the old type of fireplace or install a metal Heatilator unit. In the old type of fireplace most of the heat goes up the chimney. In the Heatilator system cold air from the floor circulates through the metal unit, is heated, and passes through registers into the room.

141

Asbestos insulation is placed around the metal unit to protect the masonry from excessive heat and to allow for expansion. This is as easily done as wrapping yourself in a blanket. (See the Heatilator illustrations on pages 143 and 144.)

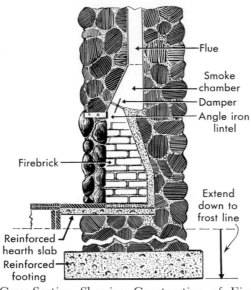

Cross-Section Showing Construction of Fireplace Without Heatilator Unit

The shape of your fireplace will be conditioned by the metal unit itself which serves as a form and a guide as you build. Remember always that the masonry must not be laid directly against the Heatilator unit because of expansion. However, the throat, smoke shelf, dimension of the opening in relation to the chimney, and the position of the damper have already been decided for you by these components already constructed and at hand. The assembly is a purely mechanical operation, and the fireplace so far as technical aspects are concerned will build itself. But your artistry and sense of balance are required to make the outer appearance of your fireplace an effective complement. The result can be just the difference between ending up with a monstrosity rather than with a pleasantly imposing hearth.

Build your fireplace of brick, marble, ceramic tile, plastic tile, or broken colored glass, if you must. But if you build it with anything but stone for a log cabin, it will be as out of place as a penguin on a desert.

In the case of a frame cabin, a brick fireplace, or a fireplace built from the other materials I have just mentioned, is not of necessity discordant. There are artistic possibilities in these materials, and I am not in the least opposed to them. But no matter what your tastes, let the final result be artistic and harmonious. If you are in doubt, take a preliminary look at what others have attempted and judge for yourself before choosing your material.

Method of Installing Heatilator Unit

For myself, whenever I begin the building of a fireplace, I enter a world where the beauty of the surfaces of stone reigns supreme. I become one with those who see this vibrant earth in the rocks of which it is composed. Perhaps because of this, when I begin the building of my stone fireplace, I think in terms of broad patterns and large surfaces.

It is only rarely that you will be lucky enough to glimpse this beauty ready-made in some abandoned quarry or exposed cliff side where the split stone is exposed to view. More often your raw material will be boulders which have little to offer in their original shape, but a blow with a 15-pound sledge may reveal a flat surface of rock lamination that will surprise you. This can also be done with a 5-pound sledge and what is called in stonework a "bull point." (See illustrations of stone tools, pages 103 and 104.)

Splitting a round boulder in two means that you gain two flat circular surfaces. A blow with a pitching chisel (again see illustrations of stone tools) along the circular edge will create a square, rectangular, or irregularly shaped surface. In the finished fireplace wall, the surface will look exactly like one side of a quarried stone. Such split boulders need only to be placed with their flat surfaces against a concrete form and concrete poured behind and between them to complete the job of masonry.

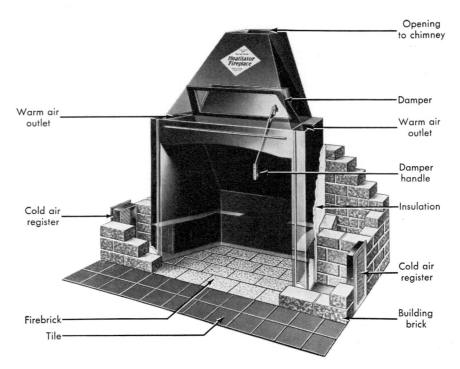

Building the Modern Fireplace with Heatilator Unit

You can save yourself a lot of work both in splitting and in hauling your boulders if you split them where you find them, and then lay them out on a flat piece of ground, or even on your cabin floor, to form the general pattern of the face of your fireplace. Square up the edges with a pitching chisel and again lay out the rock in various rough patterns until you come up with an effective combination. If you don't do so, you will end up with an unbalanced design that is a hodgepodge.

Quarry stone is laid up as masonry. There you can see as you go along what the design tends to be. In laying split boulders against a wooden form, you cannot as readily control your pattern because it is shaping up behind the "wooden curtain" of your concrete form.

So far, no emphasis has been placed on the use of whole boulders. These, of course, can be laid up in the same manner as quarried stone, using standard masonry methods, providing that no more than two courses are laid before allowing them to set for a few hours or more. Unless you find a sufficient number of boulders, all with at least one comparatively flat surface for the facing, you will find that with their bulging contours they do not give a very pleasing effect. Years ago this type of fireplace, for some reason, had great appeal. Today, with only an elementary knowledge of how to cut stone, it seems not only primitive but clumsy.

Because concrete will run, and deface your beautiful split-boulder surfaces, it is best to let the concrete set for three or four hours. Then remove the forms and rake off the concrete. You can rake out the joints too, but make up your mind whether you want "shadow joints" or a smooth face. In either event you will want to get the cement off the surfaces of the rock. A piece of shingle will serve for this scraping job, and a small wire brush is handy for the final finishing off. You can afford to be fussy about this cleaning. I find that for swabbing the stone a rag soaked in vinegar and wrung out will neutralize the cement bond on the stone, making it possible to wash off the excess cement at a later time.

Concrete for filling around the split boulders is made from one part of Portland cement and three parts of clean sharp sand, adding just enough water to make the mixture a thick, mushy consistency. For fill-in around the rock, throw in all the gravel and small rock that can be completely covered by the concrete mixture.

If you are laying up quarried stone, you will need a regular mortar mix from the lumberyard, to which you merely add sand and water. For myself, I use my own mortar mix of one part of cement, one-tenth part of hydrated lime, and three parts of sand. Both of these mortar mixes should have enough water added to make the mortar stiff enough not to be runny; otherwise it will trickle over the stone surfaces. This mortar is difficult to remove from some kinds of porous stone.

Whether you are making concrete or mortar, the ingredients are first thoroughly mixed in their dry state—and I do mean mixed. A strong back and a weak mind are assets in this mixing process. Mix until you are weary of your job, and then mix some more. You will then have a good concrete or mortar. For concrete you generally can rent a power mixer.

Earlier I mentioned the beauty of masonry done by the inexperienced hand. I need to speak a word of warning here. No matter how rough the masonry in a fireplace, a sense of balance in placing the stones must be maintained. Stones laid into the face of a fireplace without proportion, balance, and position can be ugly in appearance.

When you lay your stones out on the floor or ground for a pattern, place the large stones so that they will be at the bottom courses of your fireplace. You don't have to match stone for stone on alternate sides of your fireplace. That is not what is meant by balance. But a big stone at one side and a cluster of small stones on the other could strike a poor balance. Try a number of patterns until you find one which satisfies your sense of proportion.

The concrete slab which is the foundation of your masonry has been described. Begin your masonry by putting a trowelful or more of mortar at each corner of your slab, and set in the corner stones. These may be about the same weight but not necessarily the same shape. Continue the first course all around with fairly large stones, filling in between them with mortar, and supporting them behind with mortar and spalls (broken pieces of stone).

It is well to have the bottom of the fireplace opening above the surface of the floor, but remember that if your fireplace is too high, you won't get that nice feeling of warmth around your feet when you toast your shins. On the other hand, if you have it too low, your open-fire cooking will be performed at floor level. You can compromise by raising the hearth one course of stones, and hope to achieve a satisfactory balance.

When you know the height you want your fire, lay in firebrick as shown in the illustration on page 144. Firebrick are not the brick used in general construction, but special fire-resistant brick that will withstand enormous temperatures.

Your next operation will be to set in your metal Heatilator unit.

In the old fireplace without this unit, the only guide for the masonry was your own design for the fireplace. It was a tough masonry job for the layman. When the masonry went straight up, all was well. But the sloping of the masonry at the top of the opening was as tricky as building an igloo. Now you simply set the metal unit in place, wrap it with insulation, and lay the masonry around it.

It is well for the amateur builder to allow the first two courses of stone to set for a day before continuing on with the upper part. This will give a good support to additional masonry. This presetting up, or at least partial setting up, of the mortar should be continued throughout the construction of the fireplace, with a few courses laid each time, if boulders are used. With brick and reasonably flat stone surfaces, this is not necessary.

Raking out cement joints and cleaning stone surfaces have been mentioned. When you lay only a few courses of stone between each mortar setting, the cleaning-off job is more readily handled in the intervals, and is much less laborious. Work carefully to avoid splashing mortar and concrete on your finished work.

The fireplace illustrations and cross section should permit the reader to follow through on each course of rock, stone, or brick, and enable him to work out succeeding structural parts of the fireplace.

When you reach the chimney, again thanks to your metal unit, you can use flue-lining tile to line the chimney and guide the masonry as it goes up. The flue opening should have 15 square inches to each square foot of fireplace opening, but this can vary according to draft conditions. If the area around the cabin is open, or on a high elevation, the flue opening can be less. If the area is low and surrounded by trees, the opening should be larger.

The masonry must not be laid directly against the flue-lining tiles because expansion of the tile from the heat would crack the masonry. A cushion of asbestos insulation should first be wrapped around the flue tile, and the masonry laid against the asbestos cushion. This will allow for expansion.

There is another point to consider as you proceed with the fireplace masonry. Do you want a mantel shelf or a flush front? The mantel shelf has been referred to as a dust catcher and a catchall for small ornaments or souvenirs. But if as a good housekeeper you feel that you can take care of the dust and if your ornaments lend charm to the room, then by all means insist on a mantel shelf. Where else

Franklin Stove—Fireplace-Type Stove

could you possibly put those beautiful pieces of gray driftwood?

If your fireplace is of stone, the mantel can be of stone or a hand-hewn timber. If it is of stone, avoid smooth factory-sawed stone. Several sections of heavy quarry-run flagstone with neat joints are more pleasing to the eye.

If the timbered mantel shelf must come from the lumberyard, go to work on it with a sharp ax and dress off the surfaces with a hand finish. In this day and age you might be accused of "rigging" by doing ax work on a smooth timber, but time will take care of that.

Your hearth is a most important part of your fireplace and is worth careful attention. A mosaic of flagstone seems to work out best. Lay the flagstone in mortar with flush cement joints. (See illustration on page 151.)

Plain masonry makes an attractive chimney top, but I have a leaning toward the heavy, decorative chimney-top tile, which can be bought on special order through your lumber dealer. These are slightly ornamental, but because they are only slightly so, they finish off the chimney with a royal air.

The cabin fireplace lends itself well to the shorter wall of a

The Fireplace Stove—an Efficient Type

rectangular room, to a planned corner, or to a specially built insert —but not so well, I have found, to the long side of a room. An end wall can be a frame for the general fireplace front. Bookcases or shelves, gun racks, and other complements of decoration, especially a good outdoor painting above the mantel, lend themselves attractively and harmoniously to the fireplace wall.

When you choose the stones for your masonry, remember that to

The Prefabricated Fireplace

be effective in the general design, they should be large. A cabin fireplace is intended to appear rugged and primal, in keeping with a wood fire. Broad fireplaces with long horizontally laid stone or brick give a room the effect of width. Vertical lines, on the other hand, give the room the effect of height.

Metal Hood or Swedish-Type Fireplace—Built by the Author for His Suburban Cabin

151

Where fireplace chimneys rise above a gable-end in the cabin, a second chimney for other heating units is needed at some other point on the roof to balance the fireplace chimney, otherwise the single chimney has a tendency to give the cabin a "locomotive stack" appearance. I know of one such cabin that on a windy day seems to be going somewhere—either forward or backward.

There are other ways, if you do not wish to build a stone fireplace, to enjoy an open fire. The Franklin stove, invented by Benjamin Franklin, was a brilliant innovation in its day, and still retains its original virtues. Modifications of the Franklin stove, and modern adaptations of its principle, are now appearing on the market. They are called "Prefabricated Fireplaces," "Fireplace Hoods," "Fireplace Stoves," and other trade names.

The Franklin stove and its later innovations have a certain efficiency advantage over the conventional fireplace in that the entire unit of steel and firebrick sets out into the room for heat radiation. Heat is also radiated from the smoke pipe. These prefabricated fireplaces, hoods, and stoves can be had in various porcelain enamel colors, in black iron bronze-embellished, and in a variety of other colorful materials and designs.

While these fireplace units come complete, ready for quick installation, the creative builder can give unlimited expression to his artistic ideas by setting off the unit against a tile, brick, stone, concrete, cement-block, or other complementary wall background and base. And if some copper trim is tastefully used on a black iron unit, the general pattern can become very attractive at small cost.

For information regarding firms who make these units, or for a particular size and style, consult your heating or hardware dealer. These units can be custom-built, of course, by a sheetmetal shop if some individual design and interior scheme is to be carried out. Do not use a vent pipe less than 8 inches—preferably one of 10 inches.

The principle used in the fireplace hood has been carried out in a more elaborate way for many years, especially in Sweden and other European countries. The big hood, extending from the top of the fireplace opening to within a foot of the ceiling, naturally has the advantage of a large heat-radiating surface, and in consequence is highly efficient. This type of unit also has a built-in circulating system with cold- and warm-air returns, which adds much to its efficiency. A folding front section permits closing the fireplace opening when desired. These units, generally, are custom built. Boiler factories best handle this job.

It will have become obvious to the reader at this point that a great saving in cost can be had by substituting one or the other of these prefabricated fireplaces, fireplace hoods, or Franklin stoves, in place of the costly, conventional fireplace. At least it will supply a cheerful open fire until that day when the budget will allow the outlay for a regular fireplace.

Cabins can also be heated in the same way as the city or suburban home with oil, gas, or other types of fuel, and with thermostat controls. Also, provision can be made for installing combined heating and air-conditioning equipment. It is then largely a matter of setting the desired temperature, where it will remain the year round whether subzero or tropical temperatures prevail outdoors.

This type of heating for cabins can be less elaborate than for more formal houses. Smaller and simpler installations are usually adequate. Best for this purpose is the gas wall heater. It burns either natural or manufactured gas. Installed flat up against the wall, it requires only a 7-inch hole cut through the wall, with a copper tube connection made to an outside gas cylinder or tank. Where circulating blowers are a part of the unit, an electric connection is made. Blowers are not essential, but add to circulation in large room areas.

No stacks or chimneys are needed for these wall heaters, which greatly simplifies installation. Air from the outside is used for combustion, and the burned gases escape to the outdoors from the same general area as the air intake. Room air comes from the floor of the cabin, enters the unit near the bottom, is heated, and returns to the room at the top of the unit. The units vary in size, and also in cubic feet of heating, generally from 8,000 to 30,000 B.T.U. capacity. One or more of these units, as needed, can be installed in various rooms throughout a partitioned cabin.

In rooms where there is no suitable outside wall installation possible, or if there is objection to having the heater at the base of an outside wall, floor and space oil or gas heaters can be had.

In small cabins where the atmosphere of a kitchen wood-burning stove is desired, combination wood and gas ranges are available. In one of my single-room cabins in the North, I have installed a gas and wood range, but have provided a gas unit in one of the lid openings of the wood-burning section. I can burn wood when I choose, or gas, or both at the same time, using the wood chamber for gas heating when a steady overnight fire is required, or if I want to keep the cabin heated during an absence of several days. The gas allows the quick starting of a wood fire with full-size sticks. Both gas and wood can in this way be burned at the same time. Once the wood fire is under way, the gas can be shut off.

Manufactured gas comes in cylinders of 20 to 100 pounds, or in large tanks. The cylinders can be transported in a car, by boat or canoe, motorized toboggan, Snomobile, or plane. Several of the 100-pound tanks can be towed in the water with a boat and motor, and will float when full. Large stationary tanks are filled by tank trucks, and where this is possible the cost is considerably less. The cost of gas in the 20-pound cylinders is, of course, higher than that of the 100-pound cylinders, but easier to transport. Cabins on lake shores not accessible by road can be serviced with a truck in winter where the lake ice is of ample thickness.

The burning of wood and the control of wood stoves will be covered in Chapter 12.

A rectangular enamel-finish oil heater or wood heater that will fit alongside the gas or electric stove is sold for the kitchen and has the same attractive, streamlined appearance as a gas or electric range. These heaters have a cast-iron top surface for cooking, which offers the advantage of using the same unit for cooking and heating during cold periods. For the small cabin, these units have enough capacity for subzero heating, and because they are so readily combined with the gas or electric kitchen units they offer excellent auxiliary heating where morning and evening chill, or a sudden change in temperature, requires a fire. The wood unit of this type is excellent for burning garbage.

In regulating any heating unit, no matter how simple, especially where gas and oil are burned, thermostatic units can be installed for controlling the room temperature and for automatic control during the night. Heating firms will supply thermostat particulars for all types of furnaces or stoves used. Even the simple chicken-coop thermostat will serve, where there is no electric current and where the cabin is small.

Earlier (page 49), I pointed out that sufficient drainage facilities are not feasible in shallow dirt, bedrock areas, and that a well designed, finished, and properly ventilated outside toilet will have to replace the inside toilet. Where such outside toilets are used in cold winter regions, a gas wall heater can be installed, controlled from the cabin by an electrical circuit, and the outside toilet heated at the turn of a switch. Even the smallest-capacity wall heater will be adequate in the coldest temperature to heat the toilet during the travel time from the cabin to the toilet. A two-way switch will allow the heater to be switched off in the toilet to moderate the temperature, or make it possible to turn off the heat on leaving.

Gas or electric cooking ranges now come in combination with a refrigerator, so that cabins with limited space can save the floor area usually required for the refrigerator unit alone.

Something should be said regarding the use of portable heating units and the possible hazards of asphyxiation. Now and then, auxiliary heating is required in cabins owing to a cold, rainy period in an otherwise warm season. The practice of turning on all burners and the oven of a gas cooking range to heat up a cabin is a hazard in two ways—the oxygen in the room is burned up, and over long periods gases are emitted that can be dangerous. For ordinary cooking this does not become a problem because of the limited time such units are in operation. If emergency requires such heat, then some ventilation in the room should be provided.

Portable gasoline, oil, or gas burners should be given the same safety consideration. The broad general rule to remember is that the various heating units must either be vented with a pipe or stack leading to the outdoors, or ventilation of the room with outdoor air must be constant.

Fireplaces continually take large amounts of air from the room for combustion and draft. No matter how well a fireplace is constructed, it can filter smoke into a room unless there is a continuous replacement of air. Most cabins in the past have not been so tight but that sufficient new air could seep in through cracks and around windows and doors to replace the old air. With modern construction, weather-stripping, and calking around window and door frames, most cabins become so airtight as not to allow ample seepage for combustion and free draft. To provide an open vent directly into the room from the outside to replace room air is objectionable because it tends to chill the cabin. (On this point, see also Chapter 12 for wood stoves.) A comparatively inexpensive solution is to run a 2-inch iron pipe through the back wall of the fireplace, and into one side of the fire area, to permit outside air to serve for combustion instead of using up room air. The air that comes through this pipe, besides clearing up the smoke, is virtually a free fuel supply in the form of oxygen.

Another solution is to have your heating firm supply a commercial vent, or make one, that will enter the fireplace from the outside through the ash dump at the bottom of the fireplace. This, of course, is a more involved and costly assembly.

# 12

## Some Points on Living in a Cabin

A COMMON and well founded sentiment prevails that for solid comfort a wilderness cabin should be heated by an open wood fire. The fragrance, warmth, and cheerful glow of a wood fire impart an atmosphere to a room which can never be replaced. But what generally is overlooked is that in subzero temperatures wintering in a cabin heated entirely by wood is a major undertaking, involving a tremendous amount of hard physical labor.

In northern latitudes, to heat a log or frame cabin consisting of a medium-sized living room, a bedroom, and a kitchen requires about 14 cords of chunk wood for heating and several more of split wood for cooking. In short, somewhere between 15 and 20 cords of dry wood will have to be cut and brought to the cabin area, by one means or another, if you plan to spend a comfortable winter in the northern wilderness. This, of course, will vary according to latitude, but the above was calculated at latitude 48 in the Midwest.

The smaller the cabin, of course, the less the heating chore or cost. A common practice among some winter residents in the North is to move out of the main or larger cabin and winter in a small one-room cabin, or to close off a portion of the larger cabin during the severest part of the winter.

If birch, or even popple (especially the balm-of-Gilead popple), is available in the region, a part of the fuel supply can be green wood, which will burn once the fire is well under way. The chunks should be split in half for good results. Unless the chunks are split in half birch wood will not dry properly. Splitting releases the sap contained by the waterproof bark.

For fireplace use, the most cheerful wood to burn is hard maple. Its hot flame imparts a delightfully luminous glow over the entire room. Evergreen and other soft woods burn rather quickly, making a vast amount of difference between the fuel value of hard and soft woods. Soft woods, of course, make better kindling. Hardwoods make a hot steady fire. But the wood available in the vicinity usually decides the issue. Jackpine finds its way into most of the wood boxes in the regions where it grows because it creates a quick, active flame and makes excellent kindling.

Collecting a winter's supply of dry, standing wood usually means thorough combing of a large area. The transportation method employed in lake regions is to fasten two canoes or boats together, catamaran-fashion (the method shown on page 35 for transporting lumber), and then to load the dry logs across the gunwales. They can also be rafted and towed or driven down a river. When the logs are stacked for sawing, they soon dry off. Getting the logs to the waterfront is the big task and is nearly always necessary unless the country is very new to settlement and a large number of dead, standing trees are to be found along the shore. In areas where there are no lakes and rivers, wood is usually hauled by truck, or skidded by means of tractors or horses. Much of the wood in the Far North is hauled in by dog team, and more recently by motorized toboggan.

Logs cut in 8-foot lengths are the most easily handled for loading across two canoes, on a motorized toboggan or on a truck. Dry logs are less heavy than green cabin-building logs, and most men can handle an 8-foot dry log of average diameter, even if it has to be carried some distance to a waterfront or a truck road.

Some wood-burning cookstoves come equipped with additional grates for burning coal. The back section of these grates can be removed without tools, thereby allowing longer pieces of stovewood to be burned, and materially lightening the job of woodcutting.

Your cookstove should be set perfectly level to prevent fat from running to one side in a frying pan or cakes in the oven from becoming lopsided.

A wood-burning cookstove has a few mechanical adaptations that need to be known. There is an air draft below the firebox, a damper in the smoke vent pipe, and an oven damper. A working knowledge of these parts is necessary to obtain the most heat from the stove, to regulate the oven for baking, and to throw the heat into given areas of the top cooking surface whenever it is needed.

After the fire has been kindled, the draft, pipe damper, and oven damper are opened. While fires are generally started by pouring an ounce or two of kerosene directly on full-size stovewood, I have a campcraft prejudice against this practice. Birchbark and slender pieces of dry wood make a good starter. The dry undertwigs of spruce are a common kindling in the North. Crumpled wastepaper and slender sticks will work. Better yet, shave several small dry jackpine or other resinous pine sticks into "feather sticks" (a number of long shavings cut almost the full length of the stick). When these are ignited, lay on two or three sticks of kindling, then full-size stovewood, criss-crossed, to permit a full flow of oxygen between the wood. Allow the stovewood to burn long enough for a good start, so it will not smother and go out when you adjust the dampers.

Once the fire is well under way, and you want maximum heat, close the oven damper, and close the chimney damper part way. This circulates the fire and the heat through the stove and prevents the heat from going directly up the chimney. If the stove smokes into the room after being so regulated, open the chimney damper a little more, or close the bottom draft part way, until the smoking stops.

The oven damper is always closed when you are using the oven, because then the heat surrounds the oven uniformly before going up the chimney. To check a too rapid fire, close the air draft entirely, or use this excess heat to burn your garbage.

Heat up the oven well in advance of any baking, in order to get the heat uniform. Also, do not have too active a flame in the firebox at the time you put your bread or pies into the oven. A heavy bed of glowing ash will usually carry the heat long enough for the baking, with the addition of a single stick of wood.

While you might get by with a shorter smokestack on your cabin in some open localities, follow the rule that the top of your smokestack clears the ridge of the roof by 2 feet. This usually ensures a good draft. If not, you must increase the height of the stack.

When you start a fire in your regular winter wood heater, open the bottom draft and the chimney damper, kindle the fire, and let it get a good start. Then, close the bottom draft and partly close the chimney damper until you have a fire that suits your comfort. You can increase the heat by opening the draft and not opening the chimney damper. Then, if the stove should smoke into the room, gradually open the chimney damper until the smoke leak stops. To check the fire, close the bottom draft and partly close the damper.

Wood, unless dried under cover, is not always dry enough for an active fire when kindled. The center of the log should then be split out to obtain dry kindling, because moisture will not penetrate to the inside, even when wood has been exposed to rain for a considerable time. Once a fire is well under way, wet wood will burn if the fire is not allowed to burn down too far. To quote an old saying, "The time to put wood in the stove is when the fire is going good."

Kindling from damp wood can be obtained, once the fire is going, by drying it on the open oven door, or inside the oven. If kindling is left inside the oven to dry, the oven door should be kept partly or entirely open to allow the moisture to escape. Wood placed in an oven can ignite, and has to be watched.

Maintaining a satisfactory all-night wood fire will always present a problem unless and until you understand and adapt to your own use a principle which I shall call the "back-draft arrangement." In ordinary practice, without this back-draft arrangement, when a stove is shut down during the night, the bottom draft is closed and the chimney damper almost closed. All goes well in the stove until it has been burning for about five hours. By then, all the wood has been converted into charcoal, and is ready for dangerous combustion. The stove is apt to turn red hot, the occupants of the cabin wake up in a sweat, and the temperature in the cabin reaches 90 to 100 degrees. About the only thing to do in such an emergency is to watch the fire and surrounding area of the stove closely until the fire burns out, or to douse the flames at intervals with a single cup of water, or less.

This problem can be solved by providing a proper back-draft assembly in the vent pipe. (See illustration.) In this back-draft, you will observe a "T" joint in the pipe, running out to an elbow that carries the pipe to a point about 4 inches above the floor. In the "floor pipe" there is another damper similar to the upper damper in the smoke pipe, except that the floor damper must fit tighter, and should be made by a tinsmith to ensure a good fit. It can be installed at any convenient point in the floor pipe.

With this back-draft arrangement, the all-night-fire method is to get a good fire under way in the usual manner. Let the fire burn to a bed of ash. Fill the stove with wood—some green—solid to the top. Shut off the lower air draft entirely, and open both the vent-pipe damper and the floor-pipe damper.

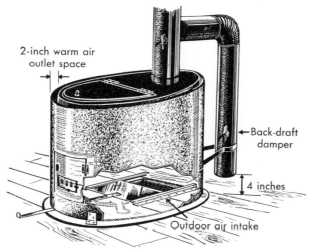

Back-Draft Stove Assembly

What happens? Instead of air being taken in through the stove from the regular draft, cold air is taken in through the floor pipe and carried up through the chimney. This gives a free draft in the chimney, the air for this draft being supplied not through the fire but through the floor pipe. The fire, being starved by a closed, regular draft, but not smothered, must get its free downdraft air from the upper part of the floor pipe. The result is that the fire burns moderately and steadily all night without trouble.

In the morning you jump out of bed, open the regular air draft in the stove, close the back-draft damper, leave the smoke-pipe damper open, put in a stick or two of wood, and jump back into bed. In a few minutes the cabin will be warm enough for you to dress and face the world.

By now you will probably have seen that the cold air being drawn from the floor creates a circulation of warm air in the room that greatly improves your general warmth and heat level.

You have now worked out an efficient system for an all-night fire. The only trouble with the arrangement up to this point is that when you use the air in the cabin for combustion in the stove, the air has to be replaced. Obviously, the air has to seep in through the cracks around the windows and doors, and through the walls. Of course, the air that comes in from the outdoors is cold. The usual way to eliminate these cold drafts is to use weatherstripping.

A better solution to this problem is to bring the cold outside air directly into the room by a vent from the outdoors, heating it so that it will expand, and thus, by creating a slight pressure in the room, reverse the direction of the air currents around the doors and windows so that the air is pushed out instead of being drawn in. The procedure is as follows:

Surround the heater, from the top edge of the stove to the floor, with a sleeve of ordinary black sheetmetal, allowing a space of about 2 inches between the sleeve and the stove. Install a cold-air register in the floor directly under the stove so that air will be brought from the outdoors up through the space between the stove and the sleeve, will be heated and flow into the room. (See illustration, page 161.) The register should be about 10 inches square, and screened to keep out insects in summer, and so constructed that you can regulate the amount of air intake. (Consult your furnace dealer for such a stock register.) At the front of the sleeve that surrounds the stove you will have to provide a door or control so that you can operate the stove draft. Because airtight stoves usually are fed with wood from the top, the surrounding sleeve does not interfere. If yours is fed from the front, you will have to supply a door in the surrounding sleeve to feed the stove.

You will have observed in Chapter 11, "Fireplaces and Other Heating Units," mention of a combination bottle-gas and wood stove, and noted the gas type of unit applied to the cooking range for continuous heating in winter regions at subzero temperatures.

In Chapter 11 methods were suggested for continuous heating with oil or gas. If facilities for continuous heating have been provided, there is, of course, no problem of the freezing of your food supplies, and such items can be stored in the cabin. An excellent place to store such foodstuffs in a cabin that has no cellar or basement is on shelves at the gable ends of the cabin, which run from wall to wall. These shelves should be from 2 to 3 feet wide; since they are above head level they take up no part of the cabin's living area. Provisions can be stored at one end, general equipment at the other. Though panel doors can be used, they make access to these gable storage areas less convenient.

If you have to be away at times from the cabin, and if continuous heat can not be maintained, the storage problem becomes more involved. Eggs, potatoes, and vegetables may be frozen solid without spoilage, if they are left frozen, and thawed just before use. Canned goods can also be frozen and used in the same way. If you are near a body of water, rather than freeze your canned goods, place them in a canvas or burlap sack, and sink it in the lake below the ice. Tether the sack to the ice with a wire. Be sure to mark the cans with a wax crayon to identify the contents, otherwise the soaking off of the labels will make every meal potluck. Also, freeze a pole into the ice to mark the exact spot.

Fresh meat is best stored in the traditional wilderness cache—a small cabinlike structure with a door, placed high on four upright poles, and reached by a removable ladder.

Just because there is a long siege of cold in the North does not mean that meat will continue to keep without some special attention. If there are periods of thaw, it is well to make an insulated meat chest so that the frozen meat can be closed in during the thaw period, and the chest left open during low temperatures. In the Far North the predator to fear most is the wolverine, whose strength is unbelievable. He will rip his way into caches, and what he does not eat he will spoil. A cache obviously should be vermin-tight to keep out mice and insects. The elevated food cache, when properly constructed, is bear-proof and wolverine-proof.

Whenever canoes or boats are used at a cabin, they should be drawn well up on the shore and then tied to some substantial mooring with lines or, what seems a poor term, "painters." Waves will create a movement that can gnaw a hole in a boat or, as often happens, cause the boat to work loose and float away. Mice will also gnaw a rope made salty by human hands, and set the boat adrift.

A cache or storage cabin is almost a necessity in the wilderness for protecting outboard motors, paddles, dog sleds, and wilderness

Elevated Cache

equipment of all kinds. Canoes, if they are too long for your cache or storage cabin should be placed high overhead on outside canoe racks to keep bears from clawing a hole in them. If the canoes are of canvas or wood, and not aluminum, they should be covered with a tarpaulin. Of course, a larger cache cabin that will store a canoe becomes a luxury well worth the expanded building budget. In cattle country, brackets and pegs will provide for storing saddles, bridles, and other such gear.

If the cabin is in the North, or at some high elevation in a mountain region, where the snowfall is heavy, much snow shoveling can be avoided by establishing snowshoe trails. These trails should be marked with evergreen branches, because a number of trips over the same route will create what is called a "snow bridge"—a compacted surface that eventually will support your weight without snowshoes. As the snow level builds up, and fresh snow hides the trail, if you have not marked it you will step off into soft snow the length of your leg, and flounder a dozen times in every mile.

Of course, you will need to shovel around your cabin door. Fortunately, you've seen to it that your door swings inward; otherwise after a blizzard you may find yourself trapped indoors. Toward spring it is wise to shovel the snow from the cabin roof, as there will be alternate periods of rain and snow when the accumulation of slush weighs tons. If you have built well, rigidly cross-bracing all rafters, these excessive weights can be ignored.

In winter you can get the water for your needs from a lake or river through the ice—unless, of course, you have a well. In the higher latitudes the ice will run from 2 to 6 feet thick. To cut through this, you will need an ice chisel. If you are far enough North, and will be cutting into ice thicker than 3 feet, it is well to obtain a special type of ice chisel from the Outpost Department of the Hudson's Bay Company. This chisel has a very wide ferrule, made to take the heavy end of a long pole. The thin end of the pole is then used as the hand grip. If the ice is not more than 3 feet thick, an ordinary fisherman's ice chisel, which can be bought at any sporting goods store, will do quite well.

The water hole must not, however, be cut too large, or it will create a hazard for anyone passing by without snowshoes who is ignorant of its whereabouts. The hole should be well marked with stakes frozen in nearby. Unless you cover the water hole after each trip for water, you will have a daily job chiseling ice. The best method is to cover the hole with evergreen boughs, and then cover the boughs with snow. Use another pole, well frozen into the ice close beside the water hole, as a marker; otherwise a heavy blow during the night may erase the spot from view. You can do your ice fishing from the same hole if it is in a place of proper depth and location for good fishing. It might seem that a box or some type of cover would be better than boughs and snow to cover the water hole. But unless the cover is a thick, heavily insulated block of material, the hole will freeze shut by morning. Snow is an excellent insulator, and boughs are light to handle.

Your cabin windows should be boarded up when you plan to be absent. The quickest way to do this is with board blinds. Since you probably don't want these blinds hinged to the cabin, they can be fastened with hooks from the inside. Blinds often discourage human prowlers, but your chief worry in the North is bear. Sometimes if he is hungry enough a bear will break in despite all your precautions, either through the roof or walls. As a rule, however, a bear becomes discouraged where there is ample protection.

Be sure that your stove is closed up when you leave, whether there is a fire in it or not. An overheated stove can burn down your cabin. A stove without a fire but with open drafts and dampers is another hazard, in that squirrels can get in through the chimney and raise havoc with your interior fittings in their attempts to get back out. They will chew up window frames and upset whatever they land on as they leap from pillar to post—not to mention leaving a deposit of soot wherever they alight!

Cabins in the Far North should have an anteroom, generally called a "storm shed," most often situated at the rear door. These storm sheds are traditional, and almost a necessity in cold climates. In your storm shed you can keep a temporary supply of wood, fuel for lamps, snowshoes, paddles, ice chisels, shovels, fishing rods, and other such items that are not left exposed to weather or are generally brought into the cabin.

In winter, firearms should not be brought from the cold to the warm indoors except when necessary. When firearms are brought indoors, allow them to reach room temperature, then wipe off the condensation with a dry cloth. Follow this with a second wiping with an oiled cloth, and reoil the lock mechanism. In an extremely cold climate, the lock mechanism should have all oil washed out with gaso-line to avoid jamming, but should be reoiled when temperatures rise. Cameras used in very cold temperatures should have the oil removed at the factory; otherwise the shutters will stick.

Do not wear your outdoor moccasins or mukluks indoors. Wearing them on a smooth, hard floor will pack and glaze the fibers, making them so slippery that when you step out into the snow and ice they will become a hazard. If you find your moccasins or mukluks have been smoothed by indoor wear, rub the bottoms with a wet rag, and during the drying process brush the bottoms, while still wet, with a coarse brush to loosen up the fibers and restore their roughness. The best footwear to use around a cabin where you are continually in and out-of-doors is a pair of lightweight four-buckle overshoes of a size, not to fit your shoes but small enough to fit over a pair of wool socks and a pair of duffel socks. This footwear is easy to get on and off. It will be necessary to cement a felt lift at the heel to make up the difference between the shoe heel and your stockinged feet. If you are to remain indoors, a pair of soft, smoke-tanned indoor-type moccasins give real comfort.*

It is generally good practice to get away from your cabin at regular intervals; otherwise you are apt to become what bushmen refer to as "bush wacky, shack happy, and bunk bound." Setting off in a canoe, on a pair of snowshoes, saddle horse, by dog team, or afoot, for a few hours daily, makes the cabin more enjoyable on your return. This is psychologically important. A trip to the trading post for mail or for some special item of food should never be considered a necessity, but a pleasure.

In the early days a famous expedition to the Arctic Ocean wintered at the upper end of Great Bear Lake at the headwaters of the Copper-mine River. Only three men were on the expedition. The system used to prevent friction and possible enervation was to assign one man to cook for a week, another to hunt game for food that week, and the third to cut wood for fuel. By rotating these chores from man to man, the three passed the winter amiably and in good spirits.

The value of owning a cabin tends to increase as our urban lives become more complex and strained. The effect of change and diversion in promoting mental and physical health is gradually becoming

* For a broad treatment of wilderness living, equipment, and wilderness foods, consult my book *The New Way of the Wilderness*, published by The Macmillan Company.

The Stockade Type of Log Cabin

better understood. A weekend, two weeks, or even a year at some outlying cabin will give you an entirely new point of view toward the business or professional life to which you must return. Such a break in routine has proved both clinically and pleasurably sound.

Whenever I drive to the city from my suburban cabin, or return from one of my wilderness cabins, I am continually reminded of a new and disturbing factor in our lives. The roads leading out of the city are grimly lined with blue signs directing us on an interminable course to nowhere—the "Evacuation Route." If the ultimate disaster ever occurs, you and I may be fortunate enough to escape with a sound body and mind. Almost certainly we shall be scattered without shelter, food, or hope, along the bleak stretches of these inhospitable highways. If this happens, our suburban cabin, or better still, our wilderness cabin, will offer us immediate shelter and a hope of survival.

Even in the peaceable but uneasy present, a cabin has much to recommend it. By virtue of social security, pensions, savings, an annuity, or some other form of financial security, most of us can look forward to full-time retirement, free of larger economic worries. But full-time retirement is a serious, difficult, and little understood undertaking and can lead to a frustration so common as to make it one of the leading problems in psychiatry and medicine today. The sudden change from a lifetime in a profession or business to a period of full-time leisure can never be easy for creatures of self-imposed habit like ourselves. It cannot be solved by the simple sub-stitution of new physical and mental activity unless these activities genuinely keep alive or, better still, stimulate our bodies and our minds.

A hobby by itself is not sufficient, if by hobby is meant a simulated interest in carpentry, for instance, or water-color painting. Such will never be an adequate substitute for what we have lost. This par-ticularly applies to full-time hunting and fishing. Very few of us will remain content, after retirement, with a life devoted to sport as a principal interest. Something more durable, enlightening, and constructive is needed.

Here I make the suggestion that the old-time unimproved log cabin has much to recommend it, if for only one reason, the admir-able routine of the daily physical tasks which living in such a cabin enjoins. The modernized cabin with its labor-saving appliances natur-ally leaves us freer of what our ancestors called "chores," but with full leisure the carrying of water from an ice-bound lake, the main-tenance of a garden, the cutting of a cord of wood are not tasks to be exactly measured in time spent or financial results. Labor-saving devices can be an actual bar to happiness in retirement. What is even more important to us is our closer awareness and our richer understanding of nature, of the flight of birds, the changes in the sky, the pattern of the stars. These wonders, contemplated from day to day, will bring us the peace from which we have been too long estranged.

To live in a wilderness cabin and achieve the fullest measure of happiness and significant living, we need to reexamine and to value more fully the durable factors of human existence.